Elisa
— from Bill & Wyn
Christmas 1977

Ghosts of Derbyshire

85p

By the same author:

DERBYSHIRE CUSTOMS

DERBYSHIRE TRADITIONS

HAUNTED DERBYSHIRE

Of related interest:

GHOSTS OF THE LAKE COUNTIES

LANCASHIRE GHOSTS

LANCASHIRE LEGENDS

LEGENDS OF THE LAKE COUNTIES

YORKSHIRE GHOSTS

YORKSHIRE MYSTERIES AND ODDITIES

Ghosts of Derbyshire

by Clarence Daniel

Dalesman Books

1977

The Dalesman Publishing Company Ltd.,
Clapham (via Lancaster), North Yorkshire.

First published 1973
Second edition 1974
Reprinted 1977

ISNB: 0 85206 233 8

Printed in Great Britain by
Galava Printing Co. Ltd., Hallam Road, Nelson, Lancashire.

Contents

The cover illustration of Chesterfield's ghostly monk (page 76) is by E. Jeffrey. The back cover photograph is of the recalcitrant skull at Flagg Hall (page 69). Photographs are on pages 33—36 and 53—56.

Introduction

ALTHOUGH I have never seen a ghost, nor had any experience of the occult or supernatural, it would be foolish of me wildly to disclaim or denounce belief in the possible existence of other dimensions in time. I have reached the conclusion, after some experiment and research, that I belong to that large category of humans who are *not* psychic. But, on the other hand, I have talked with many people who have actually seen or sensed, heard or felt with their physical senses things which seem to belong to unreality. They so seriously attest the truth of psychic happenings that it would be stupid of me to scorn their convictions and reject their beliefs. Moreover, having had a lifelong acquaintance with some of these people, I would be reproaching their integrity to doubt or dispute their statements.

What is most puzzling is the fact that the majority of the witnesses are just ordinary people who have no supersensitivity to the spirit world; people who have never attended a séance nor consulted a medium and yet who have one or more outstanding memories of incidents for which there appears to be no rational physical explanation. In every instance they refuse to believe that they have been the victims of mental trickery, illusion, hallucination, hysteria or the imagery created by an overwrought imagination.

During my unprofessional researches into this subject, I have informally interviewed a number of persons, some of whom might be embarrassed by mention of their names and places of residence, and so, in order not to betray their confidence, I use the precaution of anonymity. But, as far as I have been able to establish by such interviews, the experiences quoted are reliable and genuine. In some instances I take the liberty of naming the persons concerned as a further guarantee of integrity. Some stories are essentially second-hand and thus not so easily authenticated by personal interrogation. Others have been quoted from magazine articles and books, and in such cases the sources have usually been acknowledged.

It is not my intention to enter into any argument in favour of, or against, the truth of the stories which I have selected from a large collection, but simply to offer them—with occasional comments—for the entertainment, amusement or serious study of the reader;

and with the sincere hope that he or she will find that they help to reflect a fascinating facet of folk-lore.

The length of this work has been dictated by matching books in the series, and it has been a difficult choice to decide which stories should be excluded. Chapters dealing with supernatural songs; stories of the stately homes; Peakland poltergeists; the witness of some well-known people; odd experiences; the frock-coated phantom; etc.; have had to be withheld. Should there be a sufficient demand, however, these might be published as a supplementary volume at a later date.

1. Twelve Headless Men

WHEN I SUBMITTED a choice of four talks on county history and folk-lore to be included in the list provided by the Derbyshire Federation of Women's Institute's panel of speakers, the one entitled "Twelve Headless Men and other Derbyshire Ghost Stories" proved by far the "best seller". Its popularity ratio was overwhelming in comparison with the other three subjects, and I was frankly puzzled by this apparent abnormality of interest in a study which has roused so much scepticism and which many people—who have neither powers of supersensory perception nor personal experience of psychic phenomena—reject as superstition and poppycock. I must admit that I chose the anecdote of the twelve headless men for its titular appeal rather than for its story value. It was only the fragment of a story, but one which intrigues me as much now as when I first heard its relation from an indirect source. And I thought it would serve as a useful introduction to this chapter.

If you happen to be travelling at twilight along Shady Lane, a rather dismal stretch of road between Great Longstone and Ashford-in-the-Water, you may be rather startled to meet twelve men bearing a coffin. They will betray no surprise and probably show no hint of recognition. Nor will they offer any words of salutation or greeting; for they will be too intent upon their melancholy mission. And to assist in their proper identification, you will notice—that is if the experience has not adversely affected your powers of observation—that the men are headless and the coffin is empty!

But why an empty coffin? My guess is that the coffin is intended for the unfortunate person who meets the strange funeral cortege! No wonder the people living in the district avoid travelling down Shady Lane at dusk or dawn.

I am always perplexed by the headless state of such phantoms. It makes them so impersonal, so unrecognisable, and therefore unidentifiable by reference to old portraits, written descriptions, or personal recollections. I could well imagine any apparition connected with the Tunstead skull, for example, assuming this character and going in quest of its missing portion of anatomy. But Tunstead has no story of a headless ghost. Tradition says that on moonlight nights a phantom white horse gallops along the Manifold Valley bearing a headless rider.

One day I asked a casual acquaintance, who is a Methodist local preacher, whether he knew any ghost stories in the Youlgreave district where he lived. He was amused at the question, but after a little hesitation proceeded to relate the following experience which happened to an acquaintance for whose word he had the greatest respect. He—the local preacher—was working as a miner excavating fluorspar at a mineral outcrop at Wenley Hill. As he was going to work one day, he encountered an elderly man gathering faggots in the lane approaching Wenley Hill. Knowing that the old man was fond of a gossip, he invited him along so that they could have a chat while he proceeded with his work.

"Where are you working?" enquired the old man.

"Wenley Hill," was the reply.

"Not likely lad, Ah'm not coming up theer. It's haunted."

My informant laughed, but the old man steadfastly declined his invitation, affirming that the hill was haunted and a place of evil. Nor would he be teased or persuaded otherwise. In support of his contention, he related an incident which had happened many years ago, but which had left an enduring impression upon his mind. He and his brother were one day walking up this particular lane to attend to some cattle at the farm buildings in the corner of a nearby field. As they walked along, the figure of a man appeared and preceded them along the lane. Then, as suddenly as he had appeared, he disappeared. One minute he was visible, the next he had vanished.

"Did'st see that?" asked the brother.

"Ah did that," was the rather shaky reply.

"He'd neaw head, had he?"

"Neaw, he hadna."

Both agreed that the phantom they had seen had no head.

When the spar-miner still showed amusement and no little incredulity at the story, the old man said, "Ask Charlie B—. He knows there's summat. He never goes dahn theear after dark."

"And come to think of it," admitted my informant, "I never did see Charlie B— down there after dark."

I would be quite prepared to concede that if the evidence of psychic phenomena rested only upon individual testimony, there would be reasonable grounds for sceptical suspicion. But, when two or more people simultaneously witness the same supernormal spectacle, and their testimony agrees in every particular, then I cannot accept that they are both or all reproducing a mutual mental mirage. In the above story we have two persons who, at precisely the same moment, became aware of a spirit materialisation, and, again at the same moment, were conscious of its dissolution. Moreover they were agreed that the phantom had no visible head. To me it is an incontrovertible fact—for such instances can be multiplied

—that a spirit form can be perceived by the physical sense of sight, and does not owe its existence to a purely inward process of creative imagination.

Ald. Norman Wilson, a former chairman of Derbyshire County Council, offered to take me to Wenley Hill in his car. It was a fine afternoon in late spring. As we drove along the narrow lane, he recalled that he had often heard it said that birds never sang on Wenley Hill, which was some evidence of sinister influences and happenings. His father had also met with uncanny experiences at a barn in the vicinity, and he had heard stories of strange happenings —including the appearance of a headless dog. When we reached the haunted spot, it was bathed in the golden splendour of spring sunshine, and feathered minstrels appeared to have congregated there for a special festival of song, as though to refute the suggestion that birds never sang on Wenley Hill. Some weeks later I re-visited the place alone, crossing the fields from Youlgreave to examine the farm buildings. But they were completely empty and all was hushed and still—except for the chorus of bird song.

I like the story of a headless cavalier who sabotaged an attempt by B.B.C. technicians to make a recording of his footsteps shuffiing along a haunted corridor which was his regular "beat." The account was contained in a 1951 issue of the "Derbyshire Countryside", and was contributed by a programme producer in an article describing the difficulties of recording ghost noises for purposes of broadcasting. He wrote:

"Many attempts have been made by commentators to describe a ghost. They have crouched in moonlit corridors surrounded by recording gear, waiting, waiting . . . But never once has anything appeared. It was in Derbyshire, one Christmas before the war, that a B.B.C. commentator had a rather curious experience. Don't ask me exactly where it happened—I don't know, and the man concerned is now in Australia. If I remember rightly, it was in a large manor house in or near the Peak District that the ghost hunt was staged. The commentator was waiting for one of those rare manifestations—a ghost whose footsteps could be heard coming along a corridor. The footsteps were loud and dragging—in the best 'ghost story' tradition. A microphone was placed in the corridor, while the commentator sat with another in the ballroom, where, according to several eye-witnesses, the ghost was supposed to appear as a headless cavalier. Suddenly, the footsteps were heard . . . then they ceased. The commentator dashed over to the engineer in the next room and asked if he had recorded the footsteps all right. 'Course I haven't,' snapped the engineer, 'you switched off the mike.' The commentator denied it, but sure enough the microphone in the corridor had not only been switched off but disconnected. Both commentator and engineer swear that that microphone was connected when they left it. They had checked and double-checked it.

They connected it again, but no more footsteps were heard that night—or any other night."

It was "Granny Lowe", an Eyam octogenarian, who told me about the phantom carriage which was driven up to Leam Hall long before that mansion had been converted to supply shelter and hospitality to pilgrims touring the youth hostels of Derbyshire. As a girl, Mrs. Lowe had often accompanied her father with his greengrocery cart to the Hall, and she recalled that admission to the courtyard was by a pair of large white gates which had to be closed immediately after the entrance or exit of any vehicle. Another family link with the Hall was the fact that her husband's brother was employed there as a boy. This was her story:

One evening, in anticipation of the return of the family carriage from some excursion, the groom and his boy assistant left the stables to meet what they imagined to be the returning vehicle. Both could distinctly hear the distant sound of galloping horses and were convinced that it was their absent master and mistress returning home. According to the strict custom, the groom closed the white gates as the sound of approaching hooves came nearer and waited at the entrance to the Hall for the vehicle to stop and discharge its passengers. But, instead of the familiar coach, a strange carriage and pair appeared round the distant bend of the drive, galloping past the bewildered man and boy to disappear through the closed white gates. As the groom watched the strange happening, he felt that—instead of warm blood—a stream of glacial water was circulating through his veins and arteries, for the coachman had no head.

2. The Spectre of the Mine

From flickering tallow candle the lead miner flicks the "thief",
To rid the "spirit" splutter in his quaint and crude belief.
Then, turning quickly, down the vein he sees a pale light shine.
His heart beats fast. Is it the Spectre of the Mine?

Along the silent gallery and gripping his candle tight,
Swiftly the miner followed, but as swiftly sped the light,
Till, at the limit of the vein, it vanished without sign.
The miner's blood ran cold. It was the Spectre of the Mine.

A sudden crash and fall of rocks. The miner met his doom,
And shining ore he vainly sought now glistened on his tomb.
In lead miners' lore 'tis written, let those who can define
Why none may live that look upon the Spectre of the Mine.

THIS POEM was written by the late Mr. Henry Walker who lived in the village of Bradwell in one of the once rich lead-mining zones of the Peak District. A keen observer of the flora and fauna of the district, Mr. Walker's poetry reflects a lively interest in local history, folk-lore and tradition, and it is to be regretted that he did not make a few footnotes to his *Peakland Poems* to enlarge upon such traditions as the one above.

Like sailors, colliers and others who work in hazardous occupations, the miners were greatly influenced by superstition. When they became more enlightened and educated, they adopted a more iconoclastic attitude towards superstitions, but some of them have lingered until recent times. The names of their mines sometimes reflect this trait of character, as, for example, Hazard, Venture, Chance, Providence, Potluck, Goodluck, Never Fear, God-be-here, Perseverance and Daily Bread.

In a *Derbyshire Countryside* article dealing with lead-mines and miners, published in 1957, Mr. R. A. H. O'Neil tells of an alleged spectre photographed by speleologists during an underground operation. "Several mines were said to be haunted and one, the Magpie Mine, near Bakewell, has recently produced some evidence that it is. Just after the war a party of speleologists were exploring the mine when one of them reported that he had seen a man with a candle walking along a tunnel from which he had disappeared without trace. A photograph of another member of the party on a raft in a sough at the mine showed a second man standing, apparently, on nine feet of water. The Old Man was clearly either trying to protect his ancient rights or to help the twentieth century searchers find the ore, which is reported to be thick and pure in the main vein now 150 feet below the water level." A contributor to a 1938 issue of the same magazine stated that "Reference can still be found to a ghostly dog which prowled around old mines and soughs and was considered an ill-omen."

Nellie Kirkham, the authority on Derbyshire lead-mines and mining, tells of a ghost which haunts Hanging Flatt Mine, near Eyam. It is that of an old man who has been seen, both underground and on the surface, carrying a spade over his shoulder. He wanders among the old workings muttering to himself, but disdaining to answer those who speak to him. This mine was worked for fluorspar about the middle of this century and several men were employed in extracting the mineral. Two miners walking along the drift to start their daily work heard footsteps in the darkness behind them, and, under the impression that it was a workmate following them, made a good-humoured remark about his belated arrival. But there was no answer and the footsteps ceased.

Mrs. E. Haythornthwaite, who owns the derelict Needham's Farm perched on a limestone cliff above the mine, told me that she distinctly heard the strokes of a pick within the mine although it was actually closed at the time. When she later remarked on the happening to the miners who worked there, they expressed the conviction that she had heard the ghostly miner. He is said to have lived at the lonely farmhouse above the mine. At another mine just west of Eyam, an encouraging voice was heard urging a miner to persevere in his quest for lead. The voice persisted, "Go on, there's ore! Go on, there's ore!" But eventually the miner's patience failed and he sold his title to another miner, who, almost immediately made a rich strike of ore.

Somewhat similar to this story, we have another concerning a mine near Wirksworth which was called Stafford's Dream because of a rich vein or ore revealed in a dream to a sleeping miner named Stafford. This man amassed a modest fortune before selling his title to the mine, and this bygone epic of lead-mining history has been told in a doggerel ballad of 170 lines written by a certain Anthony Dean. Here are some extracts:

And while I slept I had a dream
Which now I tell to you
And though unlikely it may seem
Yet it did prove most true.

An aged man, whose hair like snow
Hung o'er his pale and wrinkled brow,
Bent o'er my sleeping form
And with a gesture made me rise
And follow him without surprise,
Or fear of any harm . . .

Stafford was led through the maze of underground workings until they reached a point where they could proceed no further, upon which his dream guide declared:

"*Here shalt thou find*
What thou for long hast sought,
A vein lies hid, this rock behind,
Unknown of and unsought;
A vein, whose rich and solid ore
Shall make thee be no longer poor . . ."

The next day Stafford hurried alone to his work, not having confided the nature of his dream to relatives or neighbours. As he proceeded through the workings, he became more and more excited as he recognised landmarks which he had seen in his dream, until he eventually reached the place indicated by "the ancient man" as the site where he would discover a hidden vein. Feverishly he drilled his bore-holes, stemmed them with powder, ignited the fuse and retired impatiently to await its detonation. When the haze of smoke and dust had cleared, he hurried to the spot and there—

What met my eager view?
One mass of solid silvery lead,
Along the broad vein's surface spread
Of deep and glittering blue.

3. Haunted Halls

Long years have passed, yet Wheston Hall
O'erlooks the Tor and Dale,
Where huge, fantastic rocks upreared
Defy the Winter's gale;
And rustics, clustering round the fire
Oft tell the ghostly tale.

WHESTON HALL gives one the impression that it has seen far happier days. For many years this three-storeyed mansion has dominated the tiny hamlet, clinging forlornly to memories of the pride and dignity it once possessed as the seat of John Shaw, Steward of the High Peak Courts. Since those days it has been scaled down to meet the less extravagant needs of farming families, but even before undergoing architectural surgery it had little external charm and character to claim the admiration of students of the stately home. But, perhaps as some measure of compensation, it has its stories of ghosts.

A former resident of the Hall—we will call him "Master John"—narrated to me the story of how he was visited on three successive nights by a ghostly woman. They were the first three nights he slept at the Hall after moving there with his parents in 1918, and the incidents occurred at the same time and in the same room. He affirmed that he had never seen a ghost before and had never seen one since, but he was perfectly convinced that the experience was no illusion or recurring dream.

At her first appearance, the ghost—an elderly lady dressed in poke bonnet and crinoline dress—half entered the bedroom, standing with part of her "body" hidden by the door, the edge of which she clasped with her left hand. Master John demonstrated exactly how she stood, and admitted that perspiration oozed like melting ice from every pore as the intruder gazed pensively round the room before withdrawing. The following night the incident was repeated, but he—then a sturdy youth of nineteen—buried his head beneath the bedclothes until he was convinced that the apparition had departed. When she appeared the third night, Master John was in a complete state of terror, fumbling for an electric torch which lay on the table beside his bed, and straining for words with which to challenge the unwelcome caller.

"W-w-who are y-you? W-w-w-hat d-do you w-w-want?" he stammered.

His visitor disdained to answer. Grasping the torch, he groped for the switch, and a comforting beam of light dispelled the darkness. As it probed round the room, the ghostly figure was dissolved.

The next morning Master John lost no time in dismantling his brass bedstead and transferring his belongings to another room, taking the precaution to arrange the furniture in such a manner that it would be impossible for anyone to effect an entry from the passage outside. Never again during his residence at the Hall was he disturbed by the strange visitor; but there was a sequel to her visits.

The same morning that he had flitted his belongings, an old steward in the employment of the Duke of Devonshire happened to meet Master John in a carpentry store situated immediately beneath the haunted room. Looking curiously at the youth, the old steward challenged him that he had seen the "old lady". Afraid that he might forfeit some measure of self-respect by making such an admission, Master John repeatedly denied having any knowledge of the apparition. But the old man persisted that he had seen the Old Woman of Wheston Hall and the defences of the youth completely crumbled when his accuser declared, "It's no good you denying it, Master John, I can see the ghost fright still in your face."

The old steward assured the newcomer that such appearances were by no means rare, and related various incidents and anecdotes, including one occasion when a number of farm hands and neighbours had been rudely interrupted on a winter's night while playing a hand of cards at the Hall. It was a cold Saturday night and snow lay white in the moonlit fields and lanes outside. The men were so absorbed in their game that they failed to notice that the clock fingers had crept past midnight. It was Sunday morning. Suddenly, with an inrush of cold air, the door was flung open and there on the threshold stood the angry old lady. Candles flickered, chairs and tables were overturned, cards fluttered in all directions, and the players scrambled hastily out of the room. When the men had recovered from their confusion and had summoned enough courage to look outside the still open door, they were unable to detect any sign of the old lady in the poke bonnet. Nor could they trace the print of any feet in the newly fallen snow outside.

While at Wheston Hall, Master John's father had several uncanny experiences concerning another son who was killed in the Great War, recognising his footsteps approaching the wash-house where his cycle was stored, and hearing the door opened in the night. So convincing were these happenings that Master John was repeatedly asked whether he had been to the wash-house, and each time was honestly able to give an assurance to the contrary. The night the soldier-son was killed, the father heard three distinct knocks in his bedroom—a frequent indication of impending death.

The Hall was also haunted for many years by a more material "ghost" known as "Soldier Dick"—a life-size military figure which always stood in the entrance hall. Someone told me that it was a representation of a Cromwellian soldier in armour. If this was moved from its accustomed place, it is said that misfortunes were multiplied for the occupants who fell victims to ill-health or suffered such reverses as failing crops or disease and death among their cattle. I understand that the Hall was emancipated from this tyranny by a compromise similar to that reached with Dickey o' Tunstead, in that Soldier Dick was buried in the cellar along with rubble and masonry during a reconstruction of the premises.

Highlow Hall reminds me of a veteran warrior living in uneasy retirement, brooding over past battles and bearing proud scars. Once it was the stronghold of a wealthy country squire who built a worthy mansion for each of his seven sons, and these were so strategically placed that he was able to signal to each of them from the hilltop behind his home. Now the mansion has shrivelled into a substantial farmhouse fitting into the Peakland pattern of agriculture. Two stone gateways sit astride the old grass-covered drive along which coaches and carriages once rumbled along to the rhythm of horses' hooves, but which now leads purposelessly into open fields. Television cameras have been used at Highlow Hall in an attempt to introduce its ghosts to an expectant, but disappointed, viewing audience. Although ordinary cameras have been claimed to capture spirit images otherwise invisible to the human eye, the proud ghosts of Highlow refused to be party to any publicity stunt and the séance held at the Hall provided no surprises. Highlow is said to be haunted by a White Lady who was often seen crossing the old courtyard to enter the front door and ascend the oak staircase with a rustle of silken skirts. One farm worker, who sometimes saw the phantom by moonlight, was in the habit of politely touching his cap at her approach. Once he ventured a formal remark, but received neither reply nor hint of recognition.

A carter from Dronfield, who had been delivering coals to Abney, saw a woman about 2 a.m. standing with the palms of her hands resting on the edge of the cattle trough as though contemplating her reflection in the water. Puzzled at this unusual sight at such an hour, the carter remarked on his return journey that the occupants of the Hall were astir early that morning, and was informed that the figure he had seen must have been that of the White Lady. Bumps heard from time to time on the staircase treads were said to be phantom echoes of an incident when a lady in white was murdered in one of the bedrooms and her body dragged along the landing and down the stairs to be buried in an unknown grave.

But there were ghosts at Highlow as far back as the 14th century, and the spectre of a co-heiress to the property is recorded to have predicted the exaltation of the once numerous family of Eyre—and also its total extinction. She was a daughter of the last male descendant of the Archer family who died in 1340. Both she and her sister had been secretly wooed by Nicholas Eyre, eldest son of the lord of the manor of Hope, who was a frequent visitor to Highlow. The deceitful Nicholas plighted his troth with both girls, and, when the elder found that she had been supplanted in his affections, she fled from Highlow and was never seen again—at least, not in the flesh.

Seated in the large reception hall, with its spacious staircase and oak-moulded ceiling, Nicholas was one day confronted by the ghost of his sister-in-law who cursed him for his perfidy and charged him with the responsibility of her death. Scalding words fell from her pale lips, as though the same passion and fervour which had once been interpreted in tender words, now erupted with the violence of a volcano.

"You think", she cried, "to rear up sons around you, and each of these sons to increase his lands by marriage with the best families of Derbyshire, until the heirs shall be lords of the shire. True, these sons shall be born, and their sons to the fifteenth generation. Some of their brows shall be adorned with coronets; their acres shall be by the thousands; they shall connect themselves with the best blood of the county—but my curse shall be upon them! There shall come events which shall crush determination itself, however honourable, and leave them without a rood of soil."

The Eyres did become the lords of twenty manors; they held more than 20,000 acres around Highlow, Rowtor and Hassop, and three of the female line became countesses. But the Rowtor and Hassop branches became extinct. In 1700, the Eyre of Highlow changed his name to Archer, and, after the death of John Archer, the estate was sold in 1842 by a decree of chancery to the Duke of Devonshire. And the once extensive acres have dwindled into insignificance. The curse of the phantom female has been fulfilled.

And what of Nicholas Eyre? During the year 1360, the Hall was being restored and Nicholas saw a mason loitering over his work. He flew into a rage and slew the fellow with his sword. He is said to have applied for a dispensation from the Pope and built Hathersage Church in expiation of his crime. Other snatches of stories concerning the alleged hauntings of Highlow tell of tables being mysteriously set as though for a meal prepared for unseen guests. I was told of a service of exorcism conducted by a lay preacher (whom I knew) who formerly lived at the Hall, on which occasion the spirits of a mother and child materialised at the top of the staircase.

Another story from the vicinity of Highlow was both fearful and fascinating. A certain Mr. A— used to travel in his horse-drawn trap along the road from Leadmill and past Highlow to Abney. Sometimes a phantom would appear and, taking the horse's bridle, was in the habit of leading it some distance up the road. On such occasions, the driver's dog would cower in the trap, its hair bristling with fear. When the phantom appeared on one occasion, the driver—perhaps prompted by a sudden impulse of fear, or maybe as a friendly gesture—raised his whip at the phantom, whereupon his arm fell to his side limp and useless. Nor did he ever recover from his sudden attack of paralysis.

Among the many instances of ghostly manifestation is the mysterious fact that some phantoms appear to have the faculty of intelligent conversation with humans, and are apparently quite cognizant of what is actually taking place, whereas others seem to have no consciousness of the human presence and appear to have a different dimensional existence: as, for example, the White Lady of Highlow Hall. The reason why she proffered no remark nor showed any hint of recognition was not merely her preoccupation with her own thoughts, but the fact that there was no mutual awareness. Recognition appears to have been one-sided; it was confined to the farm labourer who probably possessed the gift of psychic perception. But in the case of Nicholas Eyre and the sister-in-law whom he had jilted, death had built no barrier to intercept or prevent communication with each other, even though the ghost had entered into some experience of dual knowledge which made her equally familiar with mortal happenings and events of the yet unfulfilled future.

Moorseats, one of the seven Eyre houses around Highlow, and the "Moor House" of Charlotte Bronte's *Jane Eyre*, is said to be haunted by a White Lady seen in the house itself, in the garden, and in the orchard where she appears at twilight. It is claimed that the ghost has the facility of impersonating someone living in the house at the time of its manifestation. A small bedroom of the house is haunted by a gentle ghost which shows solicitude for the welfare of those sleeping within its walls. Occupants are asked how they are feeling, and strangers to the room have often enquired which member of the family came during the night to ask after their health and comfort. One member of the family living at Moorseats was sleeping in this particular room and was repeatedly disturbed by the entry of the ghost. Thinking that her mother must be responsible for the intrusion, she asked what she wanted, and when there was no reply the exasperated occupant censured the invader so sharply and so severely that her sleep was never again disturbed.

Mr. Brian Hickinson told me of an experience he had when

working as a painter and decorator in an upstairs corridor at Moorseats. At the time he was graining some woodwork and had left two brushes and a "kettle" unattended while he went to the kitchen for a cup of tea. When he returned to resume work, he was astonished to find that the brushes and kettle had vanished. Nor have they ever been found. The possibility of a practical joke was altogether disclaimed by the occupiers, the Misses Hodgkinsons, and the whereabouts of the lost property has remained a matter of good-humoured speculation between them and Mr. Hickinson.

I was first attracted to Heage because it is one of the few villages in Derbyshire that has either had sufficient foresight to preserve its tower windmill, or lacked the energy to pull it down when the creak of its sails finally lapsed into silence. When I first saw it, the wooden cap had been restored, but one of its six decrepit sails was firmly wedged in the branches of a tree. Yet in spite of its melancholy appearance, it had the dignity which belongs to architectural aristocracy, and gazed wistfully over the landscape as though recalling memories of past days when the sweeps of its sails momentarily patterned the sunny masonry of its tower with swift shadows. One could almost imagine the ghost of the miller standing on the brow of the hill to watch the ghosts of horse-drawn wagons trundling along dusty lanes with sacks of grain to feed into the stone jaws of the hungry mill.

Heage Hall (since converted into cottages) once had the reputation of being haunted by sinister ghosts. This reputation was actively encouraged to divert attention from the clandestine practice of two capital offences—highway robbery and forgery. The Hall was said to have been one of the hiding-places of Bracey and Bradshaw, two notorious highwaymen, and stories are told of horses being shod the reverse way to prevent detection. For many years a bedroom contained a large iron-bound chest which had belonged to Squire George Pole who lived at the Hall in its more splendid days. The chest had many locks and its owner always kept the keys on his person during the day and under his pillow at night. It contained his money and the deeds of his property, and Pole's sword and pistol always lay upon the lid. As a further precaution against theft, the door of the room was barred with iron bands. But when the chest was opened after its owner's death, the content in coin had mysteriously disappeared.

The Hall had already acquired the reputation of being haunted by Pole's wife whom he had so abused and ill-treated that she died of grief and melancholy, and he was later persuaded—much against his miserly will—to build the church at Heage in 1646 as reparation for his misdeeds. Shortly after his own death, he too was seen coursing with his dogs in the fields and riding in his coach across the

Common at Belper. He was also said to have been seen in the form of a bird, "larger than a crow", which vanished over the Hall, and at other times in the form of a "shaggard foal". Another man nearly died of fright after meeting Pole and his two dogs one night when he was returning, not from the public-house, as one might expect, but from a religious meeting. A service of exorcism was subsequently conducted by "Parson Macklin", pastor of the man's congregation, and the restless spirit was laid to rest in Dumble Hole.

The Hall later came into possession of two brothers named Shore, one of whom purchased another house in Heage to which he added a tower. This tower was always kept locked by the owner and there are grounds for believing that he spent much time secretly melting down articles of silver and gold belonging to a treasure trove he had discovered at the Hall. His secret was accidentally stumbled upon by his own wife who, visiting a jeweller's shop in Sheffield, was informed by the proprietor that he sometimes purchased gold and silver from her husband, a line of business concerning which she had no previous knowledge.

A member of the Shore family testified to the Rev. H. Eardley Field, first Vicar of Ambergate, that he was often awakened in the night by the pressure of a cold hand upon his face; a circumstance of such unpleasant frequency that he became inured to the experience and simply went off to sleep again. The same clergyman was informed by a Mrs. Agnes Stone, who had lived at the Hall until her marriage, and who died in 1927, that one of the servants was occupied upstairs in broad daylight when the apparition of Mrs. Argile—who had committed suicide in the Hall many years before—entered the room and sat at her side. The girl was so affected by shock that she was taken ill and died in six weeks' time.

Somewhat of a sensation was caused in 1956 at Overton Hall, near Ashover, when the wife of a Pentecostal pastor was reported in the Press to have left home because she complained that the 16th century hall was haunted. This thirty-roomed mansion had been variously used as a school, reformatory, conference centre and home for aged people. Once the Hall was owned and occupied by the famous naturalist Sir Joseph Banks, a President of the Royal Society, who accompanied Captain Cook on his three years' voyage to the South Seas, returning with a large collection of botanical specimens. He also took part in an expedition to Iceland for a similar purpose.

In 1887, while a tennis court was being made at the Hall, twenty-six skeletons were found buried a few inches beneath the turf, but no clothing, coins or other evidence was found to identify them or give some clue to the period when they had died. They appeared to have been buried indiscriminately, as though in haste, suggesting that they may have been the victims of plague or had died by violence. At a distance of about thirty yards, some coins were unearthed and these were dated 1742.

When I visited the Hall in 1962, much of its former glory had departed. Many of the surrounding buildings were dilapidated and there was an air of neglect which suited the mood of autumn. I learned that there had been a change of tenancy and the new owner planned a gradual renovation of the premises. In reply to my query concerning ghosts, he told me that some of the residents had spoken of the figure of a woman who was to be seen walking in the grassy forecourt, though he himself had not seen anything unusual during the few weeks he had lived at the Hall. The figure was, he understood, that of the third wife of one of the Jessops who had formerly occupied the Hall.

Taddington Hall, one of the lesser stately homes of the county, has its reminiscences and recollections of ghosts. In a series of articles on Derbyshire Homes contributed to *Derbyshire Life and Countryside*, Mr. Roy Christian recorded two stories. The first was related to him by Mr. Bill Furniss, a local farmer.

"It happened in the hard winter of 1947. At half past one on a snowy morning, Mr. Furniss had to get up to deal with a sick mare, whom he decided to move to the warmth of the Hall stables, an arrangement he had previously made with Lt.-Col. Edgar Smalley, who then lived at the Hall. The mare was reluctant to try her new quarters and made an effort to bolt out of the stable yard and back to her field across the road. It was then that Mr. Furniss discovered he had a helper. 'Whoa!' called a man's voice from the gateway, 'Whoa!' Mr. Furniss could see nobody there, and when he had finally got the mare into the stable he went back to investigate. Not only was there no sign of any man, but there were no footprints in the snow.

"The next morning Mr. Furniss heard from Lt.-Col. Smalley the story of Isaac, one of two brothers who ran a small hessian factory in what is now the Hall's saddle room and in the arched cellar below. The brothers eventually quarrelled and one day Isaac was found in the cellar with his throat cut, murdered by his brother. Since then he has haunted the Hall. It was his voice presumably that Mr. Furniss heard on that winter's morning.

"I haven't been able to check the story. Mr. Furniss could not remember the surname of the brothers nor the dates when the hessian factory was operating, and Isaac used to be a common forename in the Taddington district. But of one thing I am certain; that Mr. Furniss, a solid, responsible and likeable man, did not invent his story.

"Later from Mrs. Wilson, I learnt the story of the second ghost. It seems that a previous owner of the Hall many years ago was a farmer who invariably rode into Bakewell market every Monday on horseback and returned at dusk very much the worse for drink. But one Monday there was a slight deviation from the normal routine. The farmer's wife heard the horse enter the yard as usual, and, glancing through the window, saw her husband roll by in his usual 'market merry' state, but then, to her surprise, he walked through the door without opening it! Shortly afterwards some men arrived to say that her husband's dead body had been found at the bottom of Bakewell Hill. Ever since, his ghost has reputedly haunted the Hall at dusk on Monday, though he doesn't seem to have bothered Mrs. Wilson."

The late "Granny Lowe", an Eyam octogenarian whom I knew very well, was a person whose memory was amazingly responsive and alert. She recalled that Eyam Hall once had a ghost in its garrets. It was that of an old man who was always seen sitting at a table in one of the top-storey rooms of this Tudor-style mansion; a circumstance which resulted in the haunted chamber being always kept locked by the owners of the Hall. Another recollection was that of a white horse which was sometimes seen looking over the gate of the Garden Croft near the Hall, and this had some vague connection with a person who had been defrauded of an inheritance.

4. The Ghosts of Castleton

CASTLETON is overshadowed by the crumbling ruins of its ancient castle keep. Its limestone rocks are rifted with chasms and riddled with caves and the man-made honeycombs of lead-workings, spar-mines, subterranean streams and artificial rivers which penetrate its deepest strata. Far beneath the castle walls yawns the gloomy entrance to Peak Cavern, a place of such sinister and evil repute in the eyes of our ancestors that it was recognised as resembling a certain part of the Devil's anatomy and accordingly given a name which printers must often have hesitated, and even blushed, to set in type, and which later generations discreetly changed for one of a more refined character. Traces can still be seen of the redundant rope-walk where human spiders used to spin yarn into a range of ropes which included clothes lines and ships' cables; indeed almost anything from string to tie up the housewife's shopping to hawsers to secure the nation's cargoes of merchandise.

It is a natural corollary that a village so rich in history and folklore should have its ghosts, and we are not in the least surprised to hear the story of a jilted bride who walks along the corridor of Castle Hotel to the raftered dining-room where her wedding breakfast was prepared long ago, but where the guests never attended the cancelled reception. She had been forsaken at the altar and died of a broken heart. A maid who saw the white-clad figure gliding along the corridor to the dining-room ran screaming down the hotel stairs to pour out the incoherent story in a state of hysteria. In the days before the hotel was altered, the late Coun. T. J. J. Weaving, a prominent village personality, one evening saw a small elderly woman with grey hair and wearing a grey dress, standing at the glass-panelled door of the main bar. When he politely stepped forward to open the door for her, she completely vanished.

Shortly after becoming licensee at the hotel in 1960, Mr. Philip Williams had an experience on Halloween Night which added to the stories of ghostly visitors. Mr. and Mrs. Williams and members of the staff were tidying up before retiring to bed, and were laying the breakfast crockery for four women teachers who were guests at the hotel. Mrs. Williams suddenly remarked that she had seen the shadow of someone walking past the frosted glass window of the tap-room. Knowing that all the doors were locked, Mr. Williams concluded that his wife had either been mistaken or was the victim of some trick of her imagination. When she persisted, he decided to reassure her by making an inspection of the room, and, upon doing so, was not a little surprised to see a man standing with his back to the fire. He had greying hair, wore a blue pin-striped suit, and appeared to be between fifty and sixty years of age.

"I had never seen him before and wondered what he was doing in the hotel," said Mr. Williams during a Press interview, "but when I began to speak he completely vanished. It might sound a little far-fetched, but the man was there one moment and gone the next. My wife knew something had happened when she saw my pale face, and my heart was thumping like a drum." Accompanied by his dog, Mr. Williams made a tour of inspection of all the rooms, but there was no trace of the man in the blue pin-striped suit, and every door was locked.

A former landlady at the hotel once met a strange man on the stairs. Stepping aside to let him pass, she was amazed when the man vanished. And she described him as wearing a blue pin-striped suit! As a post-script to this story, it may be mentioned that a provincial newspaper reported a further experience of a new landlord who took over the tenancy of the hotel in the spring of 1962. He and a friend saw the misty figure of a woman proceeding along the corridor as though wading waist-deep in the floorboards. She appeared to be quite unembarrassed by this unusual handicap. Subsequent examination of the building revealed that the floor of the corridor had been raised during structural repairs, suggesting that the spectre was walking on the original floor level.

Goosehill Hall is said to have been haunted by a little lady dressed in grey who was often seen in a certain bedroom during the nineteen-thirties. Former occupants of the Hall (both reputed to be endowed with psychic powers) are also said to have witnessed the re-enactment of a tournament which originally took place in feudal days.

5. Phantom Fragrances

THE OLFACTORY sense is perhaps the last we might expect to be affected by ghostly influences, yet books dealing with supernatural events often contain stories of phantom fragrances and abstract odours. Like all other phantom phenomena, this is a complete contravention of the accepted law of cause and effect. It is a riddle concerning the chemistry of smells for which there does not appear to be an answer. I have been interested by stories concerning exquisite perfumes which have seduced the senses by their hypnotic charm, on the one hand, and the most obnoxious odours which have provoked a sense of nausea and revulsion on the other. People have testified to me of fragrances simulating the scent of herbs and flowers; of the smell of alcoholic beverages and disinfectant; even of the odour of cooking, and some haunted houses are plagued with the most disagreeable smells which have been associated with bad sanitation or decomposing vermin. Yet all these prove to be invisible effects without a visible cause!

One of these "perfume" stories also concerns a mass resurrection of spirits during the eventful year of 1745 and is alleged to have happened at Hayfield. It is actually attested by a minister of religion, the Rev. Dr. James Clegg, Presbyterian Minister of Chapel-en-le-Frith who, in a letter to a colleague, the Rev. Dr. Ebenezer Latham, described the incident (we rather suspect with tongue in cheek) as follows:

"I know you are pleased with anything curious or uncommon in Nature, and if what follows shall appear such I can assure you from Eye witnesses of the truth of every particular. In a Church at about three miles distance from us, the indecent Custom still prevails of burying the dead in the place set apart for the Devotions of the Living; yet the parish not being very populous, one would scarce imagine the Inhabitants of the grave could be strai'tned for want of room; yet it should seem so, for on the last of August, several Hundreds of Bodies rose out of the Grave in the open day in that Church, to the great astonishment and Terror of several spectators.—They deserted the Coffin, and arising out of the grave, immediately ascended directly towards Heaven, singing in Consert all along as they mounted thro' the Air; they had no winding sheets about them, yet did not appear quite naked, their Vesture seem'd streak'd with gold, interlaced with sable, skirted with white, yet thought to be exceeding light by the agility of their motions, and the swiftness of their ascent. *They left a most fragrant and delicious Odour behind them*, but were quickly out of sight, and what is become of them or in what Distant Regions of this vast System they have since fixed their Residence, no Mortal can tell.

"The Church is in Heafield, three miles from Chappell frith. 1745."

Another story concerns charming Yhelt Cottage, a four centuries' old house near Buxton, which was disturbed by ghostly manifestations due to the spirit of a nun. In an article contributed to a 1955 issue of the *Derbyshire Countryside*, Geraldine Mellor told the story of hauntings which occurred between the years 1951 and 1953.

Occupants of the house were plagued by such poltergeistic interference as crockery being rattled on the shelves; telephone pads set swinging; a warming-pan performing the motions of a pendulum, and even the electric blanket being switched off on winter nights. Strange rosy lights appeared and disappeared on the bedroom wall, and the occupants became aware of exquisite perfumes for which they knew no earthly equivalent. One night in 1953, "the ghost of a nun surrounded by a bright, unearthly illumination suddenly manifested itself as they lay in bed. She looked about twenty-eight years old and was extremely beautiful." The nervous strain suffered by the occupants of the house became such that they were recommended to enlist the services of a priest to apply the ritual of exorcism. They agreed to the suggestion, and the ghostly visitor ceased to give further trouble. The former existence of a nunnery near the cottage—several place-names confirm its situation—not only verify the story, but provoke a strong sense of curiosity as to the forgotten facts of the nun's attachment to the cottage.

One day I asked Mr. Eric Jessop whether they had any ghosts at Stoney Middleton Hall, the former vicarage which the first Lord Denman had converted into his summer residence. It was to this modest mansion that Thomas Denman, who became Lord Chief Justice in 1832 and Baron Denman of Dovedale in 1834, retired to enjoy the short periods of rest and relaxation from a busy legal life. It was he who shared with Brougham the defence of Queen Caroline against the charges of George IV. One of the ablest of Whig lawyer politicians at the time of the Reform Bill, he played a prominent part in the suppression of the slave trade and the abolition of capital punishment for forgery and other minor offences.

Although the Hall had no ghosts, Mr. Jessop told me that people sleeping in a certain bedroom were affected by strange, inexplicable smells. His daughter and a friend slept in this room on one occasion and were awakened by a mysterious smell of sulphur. It became so

Yhelt Cottage, near Buxton

Stoney Middleton Hall

strong and insufferable that they had to get up and open the window. Yet there was no fire in or anywhere near the room. Sleeping in the same room on another occasion, some friends of the Jessops became conscious of a smell as though someone was cooking bacon and eggs in the middle of the night! Not only was the room situated a considerable distance from the kitchen premises, but no meal of any sort was being prepared to account for the aroma.

After I had given a talk on Derbyshire ghost stories at Renishaw Women's Institute, several members confided uncanny experiences to the meeting, and others related some rather vague ghost stories concerning the district. The secretary of the Institute, Mrs. N. G. Fullwood, told me of an experience she had after the death of her mother. On the actual occasion of her mother's death, a combination of eucalyptus and disinfectant had been used for sanitary purposes. The resulting smell affected Mrs. Fullwood's olfactory nerve with such a sense of revulsion and nausea that she developed an aversion for this particular brand of disinfectant and would never use it afterwards for domestic purposes in her own home. Some while afterwards, while sitting in her home, Mrs. Fullwood had a strong intuition that her mother was present in the room and that by simply extending her arm she could have actually touched her. Instinctively she exclaimed, "Hello, mother!" and at the same moment became aware of an overwhelming smell of eucalyptus and disinfectant.

Stories were told of scents being noticed at Longford Hall, and of doors being opened by mysterious agencies, but the present occupier told me that he had no knowledge of such happenings.

Another story came from Dronfield and was passed on to me by a librarian who had worked in the town and who had received the few facts from a blacksmith named Mr. Markham. It concerned a "lady of sweet-smelling thyme", the scent of which herb lingered whenever she was seen and at whatever season of the year she appeared.

I am reminded of another W.I. meeting at which a member told me that her father was passionately fond of lilies of the valley. Every year, in late springtime, he never failed to visit several limestone valleys where these pearly treasures grow in profusion among the slippery screes and beneath the shade of hawthorns and other shrubs. When he died—and it was during the month of January—the bedroom was filled with the scent of lilies of the valley.

After I had talked about Derbyshire ghosts at a meeting of the Bolsover Conservative Supper Club held at the Hardwick Inn, near Hardwick Hall, a lady from Whitwell with whom I shared a table, told me of relatives whose home had a most singular case of supernatural scents. Their home was haunted by the scent of cigar smoke, although I was assured that the husband was a non-smoker. What interested me most of all was the fact that they could also see the wisp of blue smoke curling into wreaths from the invisible cigar. There was no sign of cigar or smoker—just the smell and the smoke!

These strange astral aromas appear to belong to the mysterious alchemy of psychological or supersensory perception, and yet they are recognisable by the physical sense of smell. They have not been distilled from exotically perfumed flowers to be stored in bottles or preserved in sachets. They cannot be purchased at the counter of the chemist's shop or from a perfumery store. Yet, like the phantoms which visibly materialise for a few fleeting moments, so these delectable perfumes—and more repugnant odours, too—appear to be briefly activated from the past to assail the nostrils of people living in the present.

6. The Headless Bride

"ONE EXPECTS to see naught modern at Winster; the inhabitants should wear eighteenth-century garments, and should carry lanterns and pattens to their tea-parties . . ." This was the opinion expressed by R. Murray Gilchrist, the Victorian novelist and short-story writer. And the present-day visitor to Winster will probably form the same impression, for it is a village where history seems to have called a halt and is marking time; at least in the core of cottages and houses which have congregated on the hillside during the course of centuries. The ancient brick and stone Market House still stands athwart the once cobbled main street, wearing a National Trust plaque as its badge of authority. Farmers and their wives used to trade eggs, poultry and butter in the upper storey, while lead-miners and merchants weighed out their dishes of lead below, and hucksters displayed their wares on stalls in the street outside.

Houses in Winster are in open rebellion to rubber-stamp architecture, except at the Matlock approach where modern planners have erected a council estate in semi-suburban style. Near the church is the old Dower House with quaintly carved stone posts and wrought-iron gates, and in the centre stands the Hall with its pilasters and roof-top balustrades. It was once occupied by Llewellyn Jewitt, founder and editor of *The Reliquary*. The village is proud to be the birthplace of several rural dances—the Winster Morris, Processional, Reel, Gallop and Butterfly—but its white-flannelled team of male dancers no longer performs to the jingle of ribboned bells and the melodion music of Joe Rains. Just across from the Market House is a three-storeyed house owned and occupied by Mr. Horace Johnson, who is well-known as a farmer, spar merchant, councillor, local preacher, and one of the sponsors of the pancake races held at Winster on Shrove Tuesday. The house was once a coaching inn called "The Angel", although, says Mr. Johnson, there was once little relationship between the name and the reputation of the inn, unless it referred to an angel of darkness. Many of the mullioned windows have been blocked up with masonry.

Sitting one day in a room at the top of the first flight of stairs, a lady was preoccupied with her toilet when, suddenly, her attention was diverted from her own reflection in the mirror to that of a white-clad figure slowly descending the upper flight of stairs to the

Buildings great and small. Above: Castle Hill at Bakewell where Jim Marlowe, a former butler, has often been heard walking along the corridor to the gun-room, there to obtain the weapon with which he ended his mortal days (page 58). Below: Thatched cottage at Baslow where a man was reputedly gibbeted alive for the murder of its occupant. The ghost of the murdered woman still haunts the building (page 52).

Haunted halls. Opposite, top: Flagg Hall, home for many years of a skull which refuses to be buried (page 69). Opposite, bottom: Winster Hall, from the roof of which a bride and her coachman lover leaped to their deaths. Doors, locked and chained at night, used to be found open in the morning (page 37). Above: The haunted staircase of Highlow Hall, scene of a confrontation between Nicholas Eyre and the ghost of a co-heiress whose sister he had married (page 18).

Ghostly gateways. Above: The gates of Thornbridge Hall at Shady Lane, along which may be seen a procession of twelve headless men carrying an empty coffin (page 9). Below: Wheston Hall, where on a snowy night the door was flung wide open to reveal an angry old woman standing on the threshold. But not a footprint was to be found in the newly fallen snow (page 16).

landing outside her open bedroom door. The figure was that of a young woman in the attire of a bride; but the watcher's blood turned to ice as she realised that the figure had no head! She watched through the mirror the approaching figure as it entered the room and walked unhesitatingly towards her, until with a piercing scream she fell to the floor in a dead faint. The cynic might smile and say that the figure wasn't the only bride to lose her head as well as her heart, but I had a feeling of frustration at the fact that no one could explain the reason for the bride's headless state. Had she suffered at the scaffold by the axe and block? Had she been the victim of some jealous outrage? Or was she murdered on her wedding day and mutilated by some sadistic act of surgery?

I was told that during the occupation of the old "Angel" by a previous family, doors were in the habit of opening during the night by some mysterious influence, and Mr. Johnson himself testified that he had often heard footsteps approaching the shippon and dairy. These were so realistic that on one occasion he had been in need of help with his farm work, and had called out an invitation to the passer-by to come and give a hand, but there had been no response and later enquiry revealed that none of the household had been responsible for the footsteps.

I heard that murder was believed to have been committed in the bedroom at the "Angel" and was told that a female occupant was once awakened by a feeling of strangulation, describing the sensation that "she felt as though fingers were gripping her throat."

One of Mr. Johnson's daughters and son-in-law occupied the room for a period. The husband (who has psychic susceptibilities) described to me how they both saw the handle of the door turn and a figure enter the room. The temperature suddenly dropped and the room turned cold, although it was quite a warm night. His wife's reaction was one of fear, but he felt perfectly composed and sympathetic towards the spirit which, he sensed, had not adjusted to its present environment and was still seeking the dimension of time to which it belonged. He instinctively offered a prayer for the peace and eternal repose of the restless spirit, whereupon the figure faded and the room returned to its normal temperature. It then became pervaded by such an atmosphere of peace and content that he was assured the spirit seeker had at last found its true destination in the pattern of life and death.

Perhaps the headless bride had some connection with the Hall a few paces down the street, for I was told by another Winster resident that this building had its haunted places. Doors, which have been locked and chained for added security, were found open next morning. When soldiers were billeted in the Hall during the second world war, one of them was so convinced that he had seen a ghost that he fired a revolver and the bullet was found embedded in the wooden shutters of the window!

My informant told me the sad, but by no means unusual, story of a bride who had been forbidden to marry the family coachman. Her parents refused even to consider the match because of their difference in social status, and proceeded to plan a wedding with a bridegroom of their own choice for whom the young woman could entertain neither love nor loyalty. Upon the eve of the proposed wedding, when all the preparations had been made, the reluctant bride and her true love climbed to the roof of the Hall and flung themselves over the balustrade to die clasped in each other's arms. The victims of this melodrama were buried opposite the door of Winster Church, but the wraith of the unhappy bride used to be seen in the forecourt of the Hall where she and her lover had died in their suicide pact.

During September, 1962, an appeal was made to the Sheffield branch of the Psychical Research Society to investigate the appearance of the headless ghost of a young woman seen at Dore, a suburb of Sheffield. Dore was formerly recognised as a Derbyshire village detached from Sheffield by a distance of several miles, and proud of its King's Croft where a treaty was made which changed the pattern of government in Saxon times by welding several independent kingdoms into one sovereign state. A stream forming one of its parish boundaries also had the distinction of separating Derbyshire from Yorkshire as well as dividing the Provinces of Canterbury and York. The old-world charm of the village still lingers in a few nooks and corners, although much of its rural character has been steam-rollered by the suburban development of an encroaching Sheffield. But the activities of builders, architects and estate agents have now been restrained by the fact that Dore is a fringe area of the city's green belt, and its Derbyshire frontier of fields and moorland will not be violated by any further tidal waves of modern building.

The headless woman at Dore appeared in a modern house which was built upon the site of an older one, and the story was reported in *The Star*, a Sheffield evening paper. It told how the figure was seen by a lady of 23 in the bedroom of her home at Townhead Road. This young lady was described as having had some experience as an actress, but as being then employed in the perfumery department of a Sheffield store. Asleep in her bedroom, the young lady was suddenly roused as though she had been roughly shaken to wakefulness. The time was just after midnight. The terrified watcher noted that the figure appeared to hover a few feet above the floor for almost a minute, and had such an appearance of solidity that it completely obscured a wardrobe standing in a corner of the room. The figure appeared to be about twenty years of age and was dressed in a period costume of green satin. Although physically paralysed with fear, the watcher was mentally alert and able to remember every detail of the woman's dress which she thought was typical of the Elizabethan period. She noticed that the sleeves and bodice were trimmed with coffee-coloured lace, and was particularly impressed by the hands of the phantom which were very beautiful and outstretched as though in a gesture of reassurance. But the most terrifying aspect was the absence of the head, the neck "just fading out to nothing!" After enduring the experience for what seemed an interminable length of time, the young lady mustered up sufficient strength and courage to reach the electric light switch and fled into her mother's bedroom. In a subsequent interview she declared, "The figure was as real as you or I", and added that she was powerless to scream.

The mother admitted that she knew of the alleged existence of the "Townhead Ghost", and had been warned before building the house that the site was "haunted ground." A friend informed her that he had once seen a beautiful young girl mounted on a white horse near the Townhead Farm. An official of the Psychical Research Society said she had visited the house twice and seen the young girl very plainly. She explained that the girl lived in a house on the same spot some centuries ago and, jilted by her lover, had drowned herself in a nearby pond. The same official assured the family that they would not suffer further disturbance, but the young lady of the house later claimed: "I still hear the footsteps and swishing of the dress of the ghost in my room at night. And you can hear doors opening and closing just as if the house was being lived in by someone else."

At Ashover, a headless woman used to be seen in the churchyard, and nothing would induce the villagers to go there during the hours of darkness. Her last appearance was in 1890 when she was seen standing in the north aisle of the church about 8 o' clock one evening. One is tempted to wonder whether this visitation had any connection with the following local record: "1841—John Towndrow, aged 60, farmer, of Milltown, on June 10th, murdered his wife with a hammer and cut her head off; he afterwards cut his throat. He was buried at 9 o' clock at night, after the verdict of the Jury, and put into his coffin with all his clothes on except his shoes."

It was during a discussion following upon a talk on ghosts to Birchover W.I., that I heard of what was then the most recent account of a headless ghost seen simultaneously by four occupants of a car while passing through the village of Handley. The story impressed me so much that I wrote to one of the four young ladies concerned and received the following reply:

"Dear Mr. Daniel,

Thank you for your letter received yesterday, which I found very interesting. I, and my three friends, who also saw the ghost as we were all travelling together are extremely pleased that you have taken an interest in our experience and I, personally, will do my best to give you as precise details as possible . . .

"The date on which we actually saw the ghost was Tuesday, 14th March at about 8.20 p.m. It was quite small—about the size of a child, and was dressed in an off-white smock. We couldn't see a head—just the outline and at one point it seemed to get quite clear and was waving its arms in an uncanny manner (it was as if it didn't have any joints)! I am afraid that we panicked at this point and drove off, and although we passed back that way about half an hour later there wasn't a sign of anything having been there. We went up the following night in daylight and made some enquiries, and apparently the family had gone out for the evening.

"You probably think this sounds utterly ridiculous but I can assure you that it did happen and we all four saw the spectre. I have also learned that another lady saw the ghost quite a number of years ago in almost the same spot.

Yours sincerely,

Dilys M. Twyford (Miss)."

Incidentally, when thinking of headless phantoms, I have often wondered whether the sign of the *Silent Woman*—depicting a headless female in Elizabethan costume—at Earl Sterndale perpetuates some local story of ghostly phenomena, or whether, if I may be allowed the alliteration, it is merely a morbid manifestation of masculine mockery!

The following story does not concern a headless woman, but one whose features were never clearly visible to those who saw her, so that, while each witness was agreed as to her manner of dress, none could describe any details of her face. A former Rector of Glossop and his wife were dining with Lord and Lady Howard of Glossop one day. They had recently moved into the Rectory and, during their conversation, Lady Howard casually enquired of the Rector's wife: "I wonder, Mrs. Knowles, if you have seen any ghosts at the Rectory? We have just discovered from some old papers we have found that it is supposed to be haunted by a murdered man and his murderess! A former incumbent there is believed to have been killed by his wife. They quarrelled and she pushed him down a well."

The remark had been made more in jest than in earnestness, but it explained some strange happenings which had been experienced by the new occupants of the Rectory. Mrs. Knowles had visited the Rectory while it was being prepared for their occupation, and had noticed a woman walking through the hall without speaking to anyone present. She appeared oblivious to all the activity that was taking place. Under the impression that perhaps she was helping to clean the premises, Mrs. Knowles paid little attention to her and temporarily forgot the incident. But when she saw her ascending the staircase two days after they had taken up residence, her curiosity was aroused and she decided to enquire the cause of the visit. She followed the stranger into a room at the top of the stairs, and was astounded to find it empty when she herself entered. There was no means of exit other than the door by which they had both entered.

Again, two days later, Mrs. Knowles saw the same person standing in the doorway of the basement while she was giving directions to the cook about a meal. The latter seemed to be quite oblivious of the third person, nor did Mrs. Knowles draw attention to her presence. Although she had not mentioned these experiences to her husband, Mrs. Knowles found that the Rector had become aware of the mysterious visitor, as had one of the children. One day Mrs. Knowles had invited some friends to a game of croquet and the Rector seeing (as he supposed) his wife standing on the lawn, went out to join her. As he approached, the figure moved away without betraying any hint that she was aware of his presence and he was prompted by curiosity to follow her the whole length of the garden and into the shrubbery from which there was no exit. But when he entered the shrubbery he could find no trace of the stranger.

Some days later, one of the children ran to tell his father that a woman was sitting in the dining-room. Thinking it was one of his parishioners waiting for an interview, Mr. Knowles hurried down to attend to the caller, only to find the room empty. Realising that this was no childish prank, he closely questioned the child as to the visitor's appearance and manner of dress, and was astonished to find that it was the same person he had followed into the shrubbery. Mr. Knowles now confided in his wife, finding not only that she had seen the phantom, but that her description agreed with his own and that of the child. The visitor was "tall and slim, and clad in a dark dress with a kerchief wound round her shoulders, but her face was never distinctly visible."

In the meantime the cook had become acquainted with a mysterious intruder: not a female, however, but a man in "a long black dress" who rudely disturbed the privacy of her bedroom by entering and leaning over the bed she occupied. The cook was so terrified by the experience that she refused to enter the room again, not even to pack her belongings, and forthwith handed in her notice. The following Sunday morning, while she was alone in the Rectory—the rest of the household having gone to church—the black-robed figure walked right through the kitchen. In a state of panic, the cook flung down her cooking utensils, hastily vacated the house and remained in the garden until the absent family returned from worship. The Rector closely questioned her as to the appearance and dress of the man, and was convinced that he wore the vestments of a post-Reformation priest or clergyman. It was concluded that the man was the murdered priest and the woman the wife guilty of his death.

Mention has been made of the "Silent Woman", but few people are aware that Derbyshire had another inn with a similar name and an even more sinister story. This was the "Quiet Woman" which occupied a lonely situation on the moors above Darley Dale. According to a story dating back to Elizabethan times, it was haunted by a female ghost with a reputation for arson, for the inn was several times destroyed by fire. Local legend said that the landlord was a widower who was completely under the domination of his unmarried daughter—a sullen-tempered and morose person, whose churlish behaviour led the father to adopt the dangerous part-time profession of highwayman. One evening the father waylaid and attacked a lone traveller who proved so formidable an adversary that he had to retreat to the moor with a severe injury.

The traveller proceeded to the inn where he was in the act of tethering his horse when he heard a man's groans and saw a figure stumbling along the dusky road. Withdrawing to a vantage point where he could watch the figure as it approached the inn, the traveller recognised his attacker. The door was opened by a woman holding a lamp. With a warning shout, the man dashed towards the door which was slammed shut, but not before the traveller had succeeded in wedging it with a piece of wood while he went to the rear of the inn to find another entrance. In the meantime, the desperate innkeeper had been seized with panic and had unwittingly knocked his daughter to the floor as he sought to conceal himself in the cellar. The spilled contents of the lamp became ignited, setting fire to the inn. When the daughter regained consciousness, she tried to extinguish the flames, but had to retire to the well where she helplessly watched her home gutted by fire. She did not know that her father was perishing in the blaze. When the fire had spent itself and the scorched and blackened ruins were searched, the father's body was recovered from the cellar where he had been trapped when the main roof beam had collapsed and fallen across the iron door. Shocked by this discovery, the daughter fled from the stricken scene to die of melancholy and mental derangement upon the moors where her body was later found.

The incendiary ghost of the Quiet Woman lingered around the inn, and time and again the premises were re-built only to be ravaged by fire. The last buildings are said to have been erected in 1874 after a previous fire. Even when the inn was converted into a farm, the phantom fire-raiser continued to exercise an evil spell over the property. After being used as a country club, it was again desolated by fire in 1966, and, when the owner attempted its re-building, the caravan which served as his temporary living quarters was gutted by fire! Thus, fire was the first and the final phase of this inn with its old, unhappy story.

7. Gabriel's Ghost Hounds

Oft have I heard my honoured mother say
How she hath listened to the Gabriel Hounds:
Those strange, unearthly, and mysterious sounds
Which on the ear through murkiest darkness fell:
And how, entranced by superstitious spell,
The trembling villager not seldom heard,
In the quaint notes of the nocturnal bird
Of death premonished, some sick neighbour's knell.
I, too, remember once, at midnight dark,
How these sky-yelpers startled me, and stirred
My fancy, so I could have then averred
A mimic pack of beagles low did bark.

THESE LINES were written by John Holland, the Sheffield poet, whose mother was a native of Staveley, near Chesterfield. She was evidently well acquainted with the superstitions concerning the eerie sounds attributed to the Gabriel's ghost hounds. This ominous yelping was believed to be a warning of impending doom. Another name was Rache-hounds, a rache being a medieval hound which tracked by scent. It was formerly believed that the sounds were produced by a pack of evil spirits hunting for souls condemned to eternal torture, while some claimed that they were the pathetic cries of the spirits of unbaptised infants who, not having been submitted to this religious ritual during their brief span of life, were denied an entrance into Paradise. More scientific efforts made to solve the mystery of these wailing sounds suggested that they were the cries of the bean goose made during its migratory flight. Another theory maintained that they are shrieking sounds made by a bird which soars to a great height about the close of day in summer.

In one of his *Tales and Traditions of the Peak*, William Wood tells how two young lovers—who were in danger of being thwarted in their matrimonial intentions—resorted to the use of this superstition to obtain their desired aim. The parents of the girl, whose name was Mary Bowman, were ambitious for their daughter's future welfare and encouraged the attentions of a suitor belonging to a family of some means and social standing, to the disadvantage of Birch, a local youth who had gained the affection of Mary. Having secretly taken an emetic, Mary simulated illness, and her brother and her sweetheart conspired to imitate the cries of Gabriel's Hounds outside the window of the sick chamber where she was being anxiously attended by her parents and would-be lover. When the parents heard the sounds they showed so much distress that the fickle suitor forthwith suspended his visits. The sick girl made a lightning recovery and eloped with Birch to be clandestinely—but happily—married!

Gabriel's Hounds were only identifiable by sound; never by sight. But this is not the case with ghost dogs, many of which have been both seen and heard. Some ghost dogs are friendly, while others are fearsome animals. The Barghast belongs to the latter class, and was described as a big, black animal with baleful, glaring eyes of great size, which padded noiselessly along, and could often be seen at three lane ends at twilight. It was deemed to be a wise precaution for any person meeting the barghast to "give it the wall", a phrase which implies that the animal should be given passage between the pedestrian and the wall, rather than attempting to force it to the edge of the pavement.

It is recorded that the people of Edale have seen the phantom of a black dog, particularly in the vicinity of the artificial mounds known as The Tips, and which consist of material excavated from the Cowburn Tunnel. Those who have visited Peel Castle in the Isle of Man will perhaps have heard the tales of terror told about a black dog which haunts part of the Castle. But some ghost dogs appear to be benign and affectionate creatures, manifesting the same instincts of faithfulness and attachment that they did in life. We read of the White Lady of The Hagge, near Staveley, with her white greyhound following at her heels, and of Samuel Pole, the squire of evil reputation who lived at Heage Hall, and who was often seen accompanied by his black dog.

My mother used to speak of an incident which happened to her as a young woman living at Calver. One dark night she had to pass along a lonely stretch of road known as the Brook Bottom which linked Calver with the then detached colony of Calver Bridge. As she walked timidly along this dark road, she had an intuition—imagined or otherwise—of lurking danger, but suddenly found comfort with the discovery of a friendly white dog which trotted quietly along by her side. Although she was usually afraid of animals, this canine companion inspired her with a sense of courage and dispelled the fears engendered by the dark and lonely road. When they reached the safety of cottage lights and a busier thoroughfare, to my mother's amazement, the friendly dog deserted her and passed through a solid stone wall!

I was also informed of a Methodist minister, whose business involved collecting contributions from stewards of various chapels in the circuit which he served, having a somewhat similar experience.

His routine calls were known to a number of people, and one night he was unknowingly (at the time) being followed by two unsavoury characters intent upon relieving him of the contents of the bag in which he carried the monies collected from various villages. As he walked along the dark, tree-shadowed avenue from Calver Sough to Stoney Middleton, he was joined by a large dog which followed at his heels until he reached the latter village. Fearing that he might be inadvertently attracting the dog from its home and owner, the minister used his stout walking-stick to persuade it gently to return home, when, to his astonishment, he found that the stick met with no resistance and passed through the "body" of the animal.

A phantom dog with a "pleased and friendly face" haunted Bank House in the village of Mappleton, and was sometimes seen dashing wildly round the bedroom of the Misses Edith and Cissie Robinson. It would also lie under their beds, when its breathing was quite audible, and sometimes they could hear it panting as though after exertion or as the result of heat. But the occupants of the room were never frightened or unduly disturbed by the animal's presence. In the same room was a child's cot beneath which were a number of documents and bundles of old papers, and the phantom dog was in the habit of scratching at these for a few seconds. On one occasion it was found in the attic.

A Fairfield man, on a visit to a farm three miles away, was unable to make the journey back home because of a heavy fall of snow, and was obliged to spend the night on a couch in the parlour. He was persistently disturbed by the loud whining of a dog in the room. When he complained to his host of the cause of his broken sleep, the farmer explained that the whining was that of a favourite dog which had died three years before.

An occupant of Trafalgar House, a substantial stone-built house at Burbage, near Buxton, described how "on one occasion, during the night, I heard the rushing patter of feet, as of some four-footed animal. The steps came down the passage, into my room and under my bed, where they ceased. Assuming it to be my dog, I called him sharply to come out, and when I received no response I switched on my light and looked under the bed. There was no one there. It was only then I realised that my bedroom door was shut. The sounds were far too heavy and loud for either rats or mice." In this house it was quite common for doors to open and close on their own volition, and "a friend staying in the house once saw her bedroom door open wide during the night, and was conscious of someone standing there. Supposing it to be her hostess, she said, 'Do you want anything, Mrs. H—?' There was no reply and the door slowly closed again. There was no wind, and in any case, the door had been securely closed and could not have blown open. On making enquiries next morning she found that no member of the household had entered her room the previous night."

A contributor to a 1938 issue of the *Derbyshire Countryside* wrote: "There were probably more superstitions amongst the lead-miners, but many have been lost or forgotten. Reference can still be found to a ghostly dog which prowled around old mines and soughs and was considered an ill-omen." It was probably this same dog to which J. Castle Hall refers in the appendix to his poetical work *The Astrologer's Daughter*. "Weird is the story of the Black Dog of Bradwell. Two miners who had been playing cards one Sunday were standing in the Town Gate discussing their luck. It was getting late, but the night was fine and moonlit. Just as they were about to separate for the night, although invisible to his companion, one of the men was terrified by the sudden appearance of a strange and perfectly black dog of unusual size, that came slowly up to them, but vanished under their feet. He repeatedly called his friend's attention to the dog and pointed to it, but his companion only laughed and said there was no dog. The other, however, was so assured of the vision being a judgment and an omen of evil, that he refrained himself, and sought in vain to prevent his fellow worker from going down the mine on the following day. The latter, however, went and, as in this case is well known, perished, the roof of the mine falling upon him. The survivor, it should be added, henceforth led a new and useful life, and was the means of recalling many fellow miners from the error of their ways."

8. Occult Happenings and Ordinary People

IN ORDER not to be misunderstood, I must explain that the use of the adjective "ordinary" in the title of this chapter is purely in its relationship between the people concerned and the subject under consideration. Some of the persons mentioned may be quite extra-ordinary in the possession and exercise of other gifts, but they are admittedly ignorant of the mysteries of psychic phenomena, and in general have not the least inclination or desire to develop any instincts they may have in this direction. They may perhaps be described as aliens to etherealism who have been innocently involved as spies in the spirit world.

Returning from a rabbit-shooting expedition early one morning, a friend of mine and his brother were walking leisurely up Eyam Dale with their guns tucked under their arms, when they had to leap hurriedly aside to avoid being knocked over by a cyclist who came racing down the steep gradient at breakneck speed. Turning quickly to watch the rider and to give him some candid—and no doubt, colourful—advice, both spectators were shocked to find the road completely deserted! The brothers were so convinced of the reality of the vanished cyclist that they made a search of the banks of a stream which tumbles in cascades alongside the road, thinking that he may have been pitched into the water. But the search was fruitless.

On a later occasion, one dark night, this same friend and his wife were walking along Stoney Middleton Dale in the direction of that village, when they were startled by the sudden sound of a cycle over-taking them from the rear. They could distinctly hear the swish of the rubber-tyred wheels on the road surface, the clatter of the mud-guards and rattle of the chain.

"This sounds a ramshackle bike", commented my friend, "we'd better stand on one side and let it pass", and instinctively they edged into the gutter to allow the machine to pass. At the same moment a Chesterfield service bus approaching from the opposite direction rounded a bend in the road, its headlights sweeping away the darkness, but neither of the onlookers could see either cycle or cyclist. Telling the story to workmates in the factory where he was then employed, my friend was greeted with amused and sceptical comments, until one of their number, who had been standing quietly by, remarked, "It's all right, you can laugh, but I've seen exactly the same thing." The wife testified to me that, although neither of them saw the passing cyclist, she distinctly saw his shadow and that of the cycle upon which he was mounted.

I was told of another witness who had seen the phantom cyclist. Himself a keen cyclist, he was laboriously climbing the ascent of Eyam Dale one very wet day, when to his utter astonishment, another cyclist overtook and passed him with effortless ease. What was still more astounding was the fact that, although it was pouring with rain, not a drop of moisture trickled down the cyclist's cape. It was perfectly dry! Another independent witness, who was unaware of the experiences related above, is an Eyam person whom I have known all my life. His testimony concerning the phantom cyclist was volunteered quite spontaneously while at work. One dark night he was walking up Eyam Dale and had reached the point known as Top Scrin—the same place where the cycle hurtled towards the two brothers—when he distinctly heard the swish of the rubber tyres and the frantic ringing of a bicycle bell, provoking the involuntary exclamation: "Whatever fool is this riding down here without a light?"

With muttered imprecations, which would have exorcised most spirits, he stepped hastily to the margin of the road, but the sounds failed to materialise into a visible machine, and he reached the top of the hill in record time and in a decidedly breathless state!

The dry cape recalls an incident told by the widow of a former rector of Whitwell. It concerned a wild and wintry night of rain, sleet and snow. The last bus to Chesterfield had left the official stop in Whitwell and was going towards the church when the attention of the driver was drawn to a man standing outside a cottage (now an antique shop) signalling him to stop. It was not a regulation halt, but bearing in mind the weather conditions and the fact that this was the last bus from the village, the compassionate driver stopped for the passenger. As the man entered the bus and ascended the stairs to the upper deck, the driver was more than a little surprised to note that, in spite of the weather, the man's clothes were perfectly dry. The conductress was even more surprised when she followed the passenger to collect his fare, for he was nowhere to be found. The other passengers stated that the man had gone to the rear of the bus, but a search of the seats failed to reveal his whereabouts. The experience caused the conductress to suffer a nervous illness, and she was off work for about four months.

A member of Edale W.I. told me of an unusual experience when her mother was very ill and not expected to recover. One evening the invalid expressed a wish to have a blouse made of crepe-de-chine, which material was very popular at the time. Although it was obvious that her mother would not live to wear such a garment, the daughter —an expert needlewoman—determined to satisfy this wish, and the very same night, upon returning home from visiting her mother, she got out her sewing-machine, patterns and material and began to assemble the required garment. At a certain stage in making the blouse, the foot of her machine jammed and nothing would induce it to continue its normal operation. She oiled the affected part and adopted other expedients, but the machine remained immobilised and she had to abandon her attempt until the following day. But, next morning, the village postman broke the news of her mother's death. Further conversation revealed that she had died at the exact time the sewing-machine had refused to function. So, out of curiosity, she went to the machine, turned the handle and the machine operated with its normal smoothness and freedom!

Perched on a crag of limestone overlooking several cottages and an infiltration of modern houses, the Derwentwater Arms at Calver reminds me of a miniature St. Michael's Mount from which the sea has long since receded. Its architectural appearance at the front has been changed by the reaction of a modern appendage, but the rear of the premises remain with little alteration. I was told of an incident which happened at this inn earlier this century when three ladies, including the landlady, occupied a certain bedroom. During the night, all three occupants were conscious of a presence which entered the bedroom and retired after a little while. Mr. Vic Sellers, the present landlord, told me of footsteps having been heard proceeding along a corridor at the inn. He himself was ill in hospital at the time, but the unexplained footsteps were clearly heard by members of his household.

I sometimes wonder whether the nocturnal visits had any connection with a previous landlord who was in the habit of playing practical jokes on his customers. One evening he lay stretched on the table of the parlour, asking his wife to cover him with a sheet and acquaint the regulars of his sudden death. The men were invited to view the body and expressed their condolences with the landlady, together with suitable remarks on the character of her "deceased" husband. While they were gathered round the table in sympathetic silence, the men were filled with terror and consternation when the "corpse" suddenly assumed a sitting position to prove that the landlord was very much alive and up to his usual tricks. But the next night he lay on the same table an actual corpse. He had been to Bakewell in his horse-drawn trap and, during the journey, the horse had suddenly shied and pitched the driver out of the vehicle to break his neck!

Another lady, who lives in a Derbyshire market town which I shall not name for discretionary reasons, told me of an isolated experience she had some years ago. When her husband returned from work one evening, he broke the news that a neighbouring farmer had committed suicide early that morning. She not only expressed surprise, but vehemently protested that this was impossible, for she had met the person in question hurrying up the street during the mid-morning. She had particularly noticed that he was in a state of agitation, and was impressed by the fact that his neckwear was disarranged.

The husband—a professional man—suggested that she was mistaken and that it was possibly one of the farmer's sons; but she was positive in her conviction that it was the father she had seen. She could not be bullied, teased, or otherwise persuaded to renounce this contention. On his own admission, the husband said that he personally believed—although he still argued otherwise to his wife—that she had actually seen the ghost of the dead farmer, for he had regularly supplied her with milk and eggs. His wife, to use his own expression, is a woman who has "both feet fixed firmly on the ground". And the wife, who is also a member of a profession, confessed that each recollection of the experience revives the same eerie sensation she felt when she heard that the farmer had hanged himself several hours before she saw him, dishevelled and agitated, hurrying past her in the street.

After helping with the milking at Ouslow Farm one Saturday afternoon, a Carsington man, who actually worked at the Harborough Brick Works, was cycling back to his home in the darkness. His cycle had a carbide lamp which brightly illumined the road and penetrated into the fields beyond the grass verge. Upon reaching Ouslow Hollow he instinctively jammed on his brakes to prevent colliding with a woman who, to his amazement, had entered the road from a field by passing through the solid thorn hedge. She glided across the road at a height of about six inches above the road surface, and, to the bewilderment of the watching cyclist, passed through the opposite hedge with the same ease, whereupon he mounted his machine to ride with all possible speed to his home at Carsington.

The figure was that of a middle-aged female and the style of her dress was so vividly impressed upon the cyclist's memory that he was able to describe it in exact detail to my friend, the late Mr. Frank Radford, of Brassington, even though the incident had occurred at night. He testified that she was wearing a dark, full-skirted dress with tight bodice, high collar, and short cape. Her hat was close-fitting and rather resembled a modern beret. Mr. Radford borrowed a book of theatrical costumes from the library to help the cyclist in identifying the period to which the dress belonged, and this he did without hesitation. It proved to be fashionable during the Edwardian or Victorian eras.

Elsewhere I have referred to incidents concerning "Master John" and his father. When the former was living at a farm beside the River Derwent, his father was one day walking through a hay meadow skirting the bank of the river when he noticed the overcoated figure of a man walking along the footpath a short distance ahead. Although he recognised the man by his gait, he could not recollect his name and accelerated his pace to try to overtake what he knew would be an old acquaintance. Stooping to pick up a fallen branch—to prevent possible damage to the mowing machine blade—and flinging it into the river, he was astonished to find that the figure had vanished, although it was physically impossible for him to have reached and mounted the stile into the next field. Prompted by curiosity, Master John's father went to the edge of the river bank and called out, "Are you there?" But there was no answer.

Upon reaching the farm he was informed that a certain old acquaintance had died. "That's it!" he declared with a sudden dawning of light, "I've just seen him walking along the riverside."

On another occasion Master John was returning to his farm with a horse and cart, having just crossed a large field, and was puzzled when his father accosted him to enquire the identity of a woman he had just passed near a stone water trough. He emphatically denied having met any person, but the father insisted that he had seen them pass each other at this particular spot and that the woman was dressed in black. The father was convinced that he had seen the woman, while the son was just as positive that he personally had not, and quite an argument developed concerning the mysterious woman in black. Next day, news was received of the death of a certain aunt who was immediately recognised and remembered as the woman in black.

A young man with whom I worked told me of an experience related and vouched for by his mother-in-law who lives at Hathersage. She was working at the time as domestic help for a family then living in a large house up Sheffield Road. One day, while cleaning a room, she was surprised to see an elderly man writing at a table, and later confided the experience to her employer. The latter, after hearing the description of the old man and the particular chair in which he had been seen sitting, produced a photograph, and the subject of the portrait was immediately identified as the writer at the table. It proved to be the grandfather of the lady of the house, and the chair was the one he had always occupied in life. After this family had vacated the house, the lady continued her employment in the new household, but never again saw the writer at the table. Perhaps, with the removal of family and furniture, he had followed to continue his task at the table in the comfort of his accustomed chair.

This story recalls one I heard concerning a house at Tideswell where a child, who had never seen his grandfather in the flesh, saw him as a phantom sitting in a bedside chair in which he had spent much of his later life as an invalid. The child had been put to bed in the room where the chair still remained, and had awakened with terrified cries. When his mother tried to soothe him, he pointed to the vacant chair and explained between his sobs that he didn't like the old man sitting there in the chair. The mother felt a sudden chill when she realised that the child was aware of the presence of the grandfather sitting in his usual place, and it was decided to destroy the piece of furniture which had remained as a link between the living and the dead.

Baslow has a small huddle of thatched cottages which have stubbornly refused to conform to architectural caprice and change, and their tiny windows peep defiantly from beneath beetling brows of thatch as they crouch in the snug security of their well-kept gardens. One of these cottages is occupied by a relative of mine, Mr. Edgar Osborne, a retired librarian and former archivist at Chatsworth House, who also served as churchwarden at the parish church for many years. Edgar was involved in the fierce fighting at the Battle of the Somme and other stormy epics of the Great War, and is proud of his association with the Sheffield Battalion of the Yorks and Lancs Regiment. Tradition claims that Edgar's cottage was connected with a distant tragedy which resulted in its being linked historically with the last person to be gibbeted alive in England.

Many, many years ago a tramp called at this cottage and asked for food. The mistress was in the act of cooking herself some bacon at the time and refused his request with the scathing retort that she had no food to spare for idle people. Incensed by this reply, the ruffianly fellow erupted into a violent rage, seized the woman's frying-pan and poured its boiling contents down her throat, scalding her to death. Following his arrest and trial, the man was punished for the outrage by being sentenced to be hung in chains and left upon a gibbet erected on Gibbet Moor not far from the cottage where he had so mercilessly attacked his victim. A passing traveller is said to have prolonged his existence by giving him food, but the man's agonised screams are said to have so haunted the Earl of Devonshire at nearby Chatsworth House that legislation was passed to prohibit this inhuman penalty in future.

Edgar is quite convinced that he has seen the genial-faced woman who suffered this cruel death and who continues to share the tenancy of his cottage, and describes her as wearing a close-fitting bonnet. On two occasions at least, as recently as 1972, during times of illness when Edgar was in severe pain and sleepless, the old woman has appeared at his bedside and leaned over him as though solicitous for his welfare. Although alone at the time, he had no sense of fear at her presence, and, on each occasion, the pain was instantly soothed away and he fell into a tranquil sleep as the visitor dissolved into the darkness.

The story of "Miss Tiny" interested me when I heard it from a W.I. president who had twice met this personality on the stairs of a former rectory in the south Derbyshire village in which she lives.

Hayfield church, in which spirits rose in 1745 "to the great terror of several spectators." In this view it forms a background to more substantial spirits clothed in white (page 27).

Stones

Haunted inns. Opposite, top: The Castle Inn at Castleton, where the ghosts of a jilted bride and a man in a blue pin-stripe suit have been seen (page 25). Opposite, bottom: Overlooking the Market House at Winster is the gable of a former coaching inn, The Angel, on the second floor of which a headless bride was seen (page 32). Above: The Derwentwater Arms at Calver, where a "presence" in the second floor bedroom caused guests to leave hastily.

Above: Coomb's Reservoir with Tunstead hamlet, the home of Dickey's Skull, among the trees in the background. On one occasion the skull was thrown into the reservoir and is said to have caused the death of all the fish.
Left: One of several post-cards featuring the skull in the window of Tunstead Farm (chapter 10).

The rectory had been empty for four years when the new tenants took over, and one can perhaps imagine the reason for this. Before actually taking up residence, the lady had been looking round the premises. When on the point of leaving, as she closed the door of one of the empty rooms, there was a sudden babel of excited whisperings from within, as though she was being discussed upon her departure. This happened on several other occasions when workmen had completed their jobs and she was locking up the house. Strangely enough, the prospective lady of the house did not feel in the least frightened or perturbed by these experiences and was in no wise deterred from proceeding with its occupation. Shortly after taking up residence, the lady was ascending the stairs when she met a diminutive figure dressed in grey attire with a white collar which she recognised as a female and which vanished before her eyes. A little later she made a similar encounter with the-same figure—again on the stairs which divide to lead up to rooms on either side.

Being a stranger in the village and curious to find an explanation, the lady casually enquired of the postman whether he knew of any child having died in the house. He replied that several children had lived in the house during the incumbencies of different clergy, but he had no knowledge of any child having died there. Further conversation prompted the postman to ask the reason for the inquiry, and, upon hearing the description of the slight figure, he immediately recognised that this was "Miss Tiny" who had been a member of the household of a former rector. "Miss Tiny" was so called because of her small stature which the postman recalled was due to either stunted growth or some physical deformity. Further enquiries revealed that she had occupied a bedroom at the particular angle of the stairs where past and present residents made their brief acquaintance. The occupants of the old rectory have never since seen Miss Tiny nor heard the tumult of whispering voices and they feel that the former residents are perfectly harmless and innocent of evil; but that they had such an affection for their old home as to retain a concern for its welfare and were now satisfied that the new tenants would continue the tradition of loving care they themselves had established and pursued.

9. Phantom Footsteps

At yonder lonely farmstead once, long years ago,
One Dicky Corkleg dwelt through sheen and winter's snow.
He made a solemn vow the day whereon he died,
That nought should part him from the farmstead of his pride.

And, though long years have passed of sunshine and of storm,
No eye of mortal man hath since seen Dicky's form,
But those that know avow that he is there to-day,
And that he nightly tends the flocks and serves the hay.

But, on the ink-black nights of winter's storm and blast,
There comes the sound of Dicky Corkleg trudging past,
For those that listen clearly hear the rhythmic peg
Upon the gritstone flags of Dicky's wooden leg.

THIS POEM, entitled "Dicky Corkleg", is one of the *Peakland Poems* written by Henry Walker, the Bradwell poet. Although there is no explanatory footnote to help us locate the farm or identify the farmer, we may well imagine that the verses were inspired by some personality who lived in the district. Footsteps are among the most common of ghostly manifestations. People who do not possess the rare faculty of "second sight", and who have never seen a phantom, can often testify to having distinctly heard footsteps; sounds which correspond exactly with the measured tread of human beings, but which have no apparent relationship to any mortals.

Mr. and Mrs. A. Shooter and their son, Michael, were watching a popular television programme one Saturday afternoon when I called to enquire whether they could confirm the story of a ghost which haunts Castle Hill, the boarding-house for resident pupils of Lady Manners School, Bakewell, where Mr. Shooter is a member of the teaching staff. He was also the housemaster at Castle Hill. The house is a dignified and solid example of Georgian architecture built on the slope of a hill crowned with earthworks which are believed to mark the site of the burgh, or fortress, erected by Edward the Elder in 924 A.D. to stem the tide of Danish invasion. The incident is recorded in the Saxon Chronicle and such place-names as "Castle-field", "Warden-field" and "Courtyard" linger to confirm the claim.

Nearby is the ice-house where, in later times, slabs of winter ice used to be kept by means of underground storage between layers of bracken for domestic use in summer months.

Mr. and Mrs. Shooter interrupted their viewing and invited me into the lounge, where they told me—with hints of sceptical good humour from Mr. Shooter, who had never heard or seen anything out of the ordinary—what they knew of Jim Marlowe, a butler who committed suicide by shooting himself in the butler's pantry to escape the reproaches of a nagging wife. It happened on a Friday many years ago, and it is on this same night of the week that the reincarnated butler can still be heard leaving the pantry, closing the door behind him, treading along the corridor and up a flight of stairs to the former gun-room—doubtless to choose the suicide weapon. There is a loose board at the threshold of this door and invariably it is heard to creak beneath the weight of the phantom's footstep. Then he is heard retreating to the pantry where the door is closed again. I was hoping that the story would end with the report of a gun; but no, only the footsteps patrolling the corridor and climbing the stairs, the creaking of a floorboard, and the opening and closing of two doors keeps alive the memory of Jim Marlowe.

About 9 p.m. each evening during a certain season of the year, I was told that the occupants of Mount Pleasant Farm, Fritchley, listen for the sound of hob-nailed boots approaching their door. The farmer has often lain in wait, crept to the door and suddenly flung it open only to find no sign of an intruder. He has even kept vigil with a shot-gun, but when the door has been opened the mysterious footsteps have ceased.

Another farmer at Gratton (once noted for its cheeses) became so reconciled to approaching footsteps and a knock on the door, that he advised the tenants who succeeded him at the farm not to answer the door unless the knock was repeated. He explained that it was only a former tenant who couldn't settle in his grave! But I was informed that these particular footsteps are the grim sequel to a triple tragedy. An occupant of the farm killed his wife and her lover, and then took his own life. A soldier-son was home on leave at this farm during the Great War, and one day heard the sound of approaching hob-nailed boots and a sharp rap on the door. Upon opening the door he was astounded not to find anyone standing on the threshold. When he mentioned the matter to his father, he was advised always to wait for the second knock, the explanation being that a single knock indicated that the caller was only "Old Sheldon." He was the former tenant who had been accused of a double murder, but never proved guilty by criminal proceedings.

A man named Darbyshire had lodged with the Sheldons and had aroused—wittingly or unwittingly—the husband's jealousy. It was further alleged that the latter had more than once threatened to take the lodger's life. One night Darbyshire returned from the

"Nelson's Arms" at Elton in his usual state of inebriation, singing a popular song ironically entitled "Don't bury me deep", and was later found dead at the bottom of a flight of steps leading to a chamber where he was accustomed to sleep when locked out at the farm—a not altogether infrequent happening. Sheldon's wife was later burnt to death and it was suspected that he had pushed her onto the fire, although no proof was found to support the allegation and he was exonerated from blame. Later he committed suicide. And still he returns to the scene of tragedy, walking with heavy tread, knocking upon the door, but never crossing the threshold of his old home.

When I broached the subject as to whether the rectory in our historic village of Eyam was haunted, the rector was reluctant to confirm or deny that this then rambling mansion (it has since been partially re-built) had any ghosts. I had been assured by a parishioner that occupants of the rectory had heard the whisper of ghostly gowns and had actually seen Mrs. Catherine Mompesson who died there during the Plague of 1665-6. The rector told me that mysterious happenings had occurred. Sometimes, when entertaining guests, he and his wife had been asked whether someone had been ill in the night, because the visitors had heard footsteps passing along the corridor, and doors being opened and closed. He and his wife had heard similar movements: footsteps, doors closing, and sounds resembling the rustle of feminine dresses. A former maid at the rectory met, as she supposed, Mrs. Mompesson ascending the back stairs, and described her as wearing a large hat.

Incidentally, the rectory was once occupied by a Dowager Duchess of Devonshire, who wore fashionable millinery creations which were so exaggerated that the doorway had to be enlarged to permit her egress and entry without the indignity of having to stoop to prevent her head-dress from being dislodged. The rectory was also the birthplace of Anna Seward, who became renowned for her poetry as the "Swan of Lichfield." Although she left Eyam in girlhood, Miss Seward was in the habit of making an annual pilgrimage to her native village, on which occasions she wrote poems to commemorate her visits.

Sounds were the only recognisable features of the ghosts which figured in the foregoing stories, and there were no visible means of identification. But in the following story told by R. Evans in an article printed in a 1954 issue of the *Derbyshire Countryside*, we find that acoustical evidence was noticeably absent. The writer related a number of anecdotes concerning Bradwell, and tells of an uncle "who often went out early on summer mornings into the fields. His way lay by a narrow lane between high walls. Some distance along, projecting stones in one of the walls formed a stile, and on the other side lay fields. When he reached the lane he noticed a woman walking ahead of him. He soon gained on her, and thought it strange that her feet made no sound, although the way was rough and stony.

"She mounted the stile before him. He followed, and at the top, as he looked down into the fields, was amazed that the woman had vanished. Terror seized him, and he leaped back into the lane and fled home, never again to go out alone to those fields in the dim light of dawn while others slept."

For a number of years I was unaware of footsteps being heard by my own relatives in Eyam. My cousin, Mrs. R. Blackwell, and her husband and family used to hear the footsteps approaching their cottage, following which the door would be unlatched and swung open. But the footsteps never crossed the threshold. The occurrence was so frequent—but not at regular intervals—that the invisible visitor was regarded as somewhat of a nuisance and my cousin often remarked with impatience, "I wish you'd come in and close the door." But the invitation was never accepted and the door was still thoughtlessly left open. When it was decided to enlarge the cottage, the usual doorway was sealed up and a new entrance made. This alteration did not altogether put the unseen caller off his stride, but confused him to the extent that he now proceeds past the house and continues down the garden path.

I have read of phantom footprints in newly fallen snow, or of their absence to explain the passing of a ghost, but perhaps a more intriguing story concerns an avenue of trees not far from Hardwick Hall. The story, of the truth of which I was given a sincere assurance, recalls an autumn day when a man and his dog were walking along the lane which was littered ankle deep with drifts of decaying leaves fallen from the trees on either side. The day was still, except for the crisp sound of leaves as they gently fluttered to the ground and lay unruffled by any breath of wind. Suddenly the dog began to behave in a strange manner, recoiling as though from some hidden source of danger and cringing with obvious fright. Then the owner of the dog saw that the carpet of leaves was being stirred by invisible feet walking along the avenue, each step causing a fresh disturbance as the unseen pedestrian proceeded on his journey. And every effort to persuade the dog to continue along the haunted lane was in vain.

10. Dickey o' Tunstead

IF ANY SPECTRE might be deemed worthy of a posthumous knighthood, it would surely be Dickey o'Tunstead. His services to the community have been many and varied, for he has ever steadfastly championed the right and just as resolutely rebuked and resisted the wrong. And if it were not for the risk of infringing the copyright claimed for the Jolly Roger, the College of Heralds might be persuaded to devise a coat-of-arms incorporating similar symbolism for Sir Richard of Tunstead.

Dickey o' Tunstead is a Goliath among ghosts, standing head and shoulders above the multitude of his comrades who haunt the mansions and manor-houses, fields and farms, cottages and castles of Derbyshire. But perhaps "head and shoulders" is an unfortunate choice of phraseology, for Dickey had no shoulders; only a head. We have many stories of headless men, but this is the story of a manless head. When or how he became detached from the rest of his mortal remains is an unsolved mystery, yet for 350 years he has persistently refused the hospitality of the grave, rejecting the services of the sexton's spade, and preferring to cultivate a much stronger attachment to a farmhouse than to the body which gave him support in life.

Dickey is a skull which has attained such celebrity that I might be tempted to call him—for everyone uses the personal pronoun—the Eighth Wonder of the Peak. His story has been told in prose and in poetry, and even through the medium of dramatic art. At least two poems—one by Samuel Laycock, the Lancashire dialect poet—have been composed to tell his story and some of his many exploits. For many years Dickey has been a source of contention and controversy. Some people have believed implicitly in the tales of miracle and mystery; others have dismissed them as instances of pure coincidence or the fabrication of superstitious people. Yet the very existence of the skull through three and a half centuries of indifferent usage is a measure of proof that the stories must have some foundation in fact.

At one time visitors to the district could purchase postcards with photographs of the "miraculous skull" and giving a few particulars of its association with a farmhouse overlooking the Coomb's

Reservoir between Chapel-en-le-Frith and Whaley Bridge. Tenants of the farm who treated the skull with proper respect found it a talisman against evil and misfortune; while those who handled it with abuse inevitably suffered ill-effects. During one period of its history the skull was nailed to a rafter in the house-place ,and for a while it was kept in a cheese-vat in a staircase window. One of the panes in this window had the reputation of being persistently displaced as though the skull required more ventilation, and, upon being reglazed, the pane was invariably found next morning lying undamaged on the grass outside.

It can be well imagined that the prospect of sharing a house with such a biological curiosity was repellent to some tenants; others considered it a breach of decency; while there were those who refused to countenance such superstitious nonsense at any cost. But, one after another, they changed their minds—however reluctantly—and accepted Dickey as a member of the family. For whenever it has been removed from the premises, such disturbances have been created that the defaulting tenants have lost no time in recovering and restoring the insulted skull to the farm.

During its long association with Tunstead Farm, the skull has been discarded by several farmers as an object of superstition. But during its absence cattle strayed away or died of strange diseases, crops failed, accidents occurred and misfortunes were generally multiplied. Not only the tenants, but the cattle and crops, it would appear, lay within the shadow of a sinister influence—the curse of Dickey's skull.

Once it was thrown into the Coomb's Reservoir, but the fish died; twice it was buried in Chapel-en-le-Frith churchyard, but hurriedly exhumed each time; it was contemptuously flung into the river and fished out again in a desperate hurry. While the farmhouse was being re-built, the skull was irreverently buried in a manure-heap, but the workmen were persistently hindered, finding the previous day's work undone when they returned next morning. In addition to this frustration of their work, the men complained that as they hewed and hammered, they could distinctly hear low, unearthly moans. When the skull was disinterred and restored to a temporary place on one of the couple-beams in the barn, the work proceeded normally. But, at the "rearing supper" to mark completion of the work, there was no peace until Dickey had been brought back and restored to a position of honour in the farmhouse. Yet in spite of its many adventures and adversities, tradition claimed that the skull was "impervious to decay and no dust would ever settle on it." One writer asserted that the spectre of a lady in a black silken dress and a phantom dog were associated with the hauntings.

Dickey was never what one might call malicious or vindictive. He could even appreciate a joke, for one man told me that, as a youth, he and several friends used the shallow cranium for the purpose of drinking water, reminding one of the grim chalice used by Lord Byron and his friends. The risk of retribution to the youths was indeed great, but I was assured that none of them suffered any ill effects. Perhaps Dickey remembered that he had once been young and irresponsible!

Hutchinson, in his *Tour of the Peak* (1897) wrote: "Having heard a singular account of a human skull (and of the supernatural powers attributed to it) being preserved in a house at Tunstead . . . curiosity induced me to deviate a little for the purpose of making some inquiries. . . . That there are three parts of a human skull in the house is certain, and which I traced to have remained on the premises for near two centuries past during all the revolutions of owners and tenants in that time.

"As to the truth of the supernatural appearances . . . a Mr. Adam Fox, who was brought up in the house, has not only heard singular noises, and observed very singular circumstances, but can produce fifty persons within the parish who have seen an apparition at this place. He has often found the doors opening to his hand, the servants have been repeatedly called up of a morning, many good offices have been done by the apparition at different times, and, in fact, it is looked upon more as a guardian spirit than a terror to the family, never disturbing them but in case of an approaching death of a relation or neighbour, and showing its resentment only when spoken of with disrespect, or when its own awful memorial of mortality is removed. Twice within the memory of man the skull has been taken from the premises—once on building the present house on the site of the old one, and another time when it was buried in Chapel churchyard—but there was no peace! no rest! it must be replaced!"

As Hutchinson says, farmers who respected the skull and treated it with due reverence, were rewarded by many useful services. Servants were summoned at an early hour, if needed; horses were harnessed in preparation for journeys; warning was given in the event of burglary, or such emergency as illness; attention was drawn to calving cows, and one farmer was roused from sleep to prevent a cow from being accidentally strangled by a chain. Mr. J. Bramwell, another former tenant, averred that he would rather have suffered the loss of his best cow than be deprived of the services of the skull.

One night a thief was caught in the act of stealing potatoes from the garden. He had filled his sack and hoisted it upon his shoulder, but, when he attempted to move, he found himself utterly powerless to stir a limb. Meanwhile, the doors of the farm were shaken violently and crockery rattled on the shelves until the sleeping household was awakened and the thief captured. Passing down the lane near the farm, another man who was in charge of a corn-laden waggon, noticed a light in the window occupied by the skull and made a derogatory remark about Dickey going to bed, reinforcing his comment with an oath. Instantly the waggon was overturned and, crestfallen and much discomfited, the fellow had to go in search for helpers to right his capsized vehicle.

The perversity of Dickey is amazingly and amusingly illustrated by G. Le Blanc Smith in an article printed in the second volume of the *Reliquary and Illustrated Antiquary* which, incidentally, contains a photograph of both the skull and Tunstead Farm. The writer believed that it was only the second time that the skull had been photographed, and permission was only granted after a serious and prolonged discussion between the farmer and his wife who were uncertain as to the possible reactions of Dickey. The above writer tells the following incredible story. One of three labourers anxious to obtain casual employment during the hay harvest, applied to a Mr. Dixon, the contemporary owner of the farm. He was supplied with a scythe and whetstone, and given instructions to mow a "swath" through a large meadow of ripening grass. Anxious to make a good impression on his prospective employer, the man sharpened his scythe and proceeded to cut a lane deftly through the grass, not looking back until he had reached the other side. When he did so, he found to his amazement that the grass had returned to the vertical and there were no signs of it having been cut or even bruised at the bottom! The man complained to the farmer, but Mr. Dixon was quite unperturbed by the fact and explained that Dickey had either been upset by some trivial matter, or thought that the grass was not yet ready for mowing. Although the labourer was anxious to find employment, he declined the situation offered by Mr. Dixon.

Mr. Smith described the skull as "an uninviting looking object, consisting of three fragments, two parietal and one clavical. In colour he is a rich shade of olive green, shaded at the edges with brown and white spots; he looks so very innocent that all the tales they tell of him seem as though they must be gross libels."

The most outstanding achievement attributed to Dickey was his victory over the London & North Western Railway engineers who, despite the farmer's objections, planned to carry a line across a field belonging to the farm. A bridge and embankment were necessary to complete the project, but, owing to the treacherous and unstable nature of the ground, the workmen could not prepare a satisfactory foundation. After the work had been repeatedly brought to a standstill, it was found impossible to proceed and the original route had to be modified to avoid the bewitched terrain.

In a contribution to *The Reliquary* written towards the close of last century, William Bennett described how the railway company intended to "cross Coombs Valley to Chapel-en-le-Frith station by a high embankment, and an archway over the highway. The embankment was formed, and a stately arch erected; but they were not out of the hands of the contractors before the arch rapidly sank into the earth, its walls were riven and dislocated, and the ground at each end of the archway thrown up into large mounds. Every effort was made to overcome the difficulty and restore the fabric, and a very large amount was expended for that purpose, but without avail. Either the ground was naturally a quicksand which swallowed up all material, or (according to the neighbourhood), Dickey would not have the archway in that position.

"The Railway Company and contractors battled with the malign power a long time, but were eventually obliged to give way, and not only to remove their bridge some distance, but form a new highway at a great expense for upwards of quarter-of-a-mile. When this alternative (which made a new and very handsome road into the Coombes) was completed, Dickey appears to have been appeased; and the new road and bridge stand a proud monument to his engineering taste and determined opposition to the erection of a bridge upon a swamp, which might have endangered the safety of the Queen's lieges. We cannot help thinking, however, that the Railway Company would have been better satisfied if he had remained quiet in the chimney-corner." It was this particular incident which inspired Samuel Laycock's dialect poem beginning with the verse:

Neaw, Dickie, be quiet wi' thee, lad,
An' let navvies an' railways a' be;
Mon tha shouldn't do soa, its too bad,
What harm are they doin' to thee?
Deed folk shouldn't meddle at o',
But leov o' these matters to th' wick;
They'll see they're done gradely, aw know—
Dos' t' yer what aw say to thee, Dick?

William Bennett also wrote a ballad incorporating considerable research into the traditions and established facts concerning Ned Dickson (once believed to be the original owner of the skull) who fought in France during the Huguenot Wars. At the Battle of Ivry, Dickson distinguished himself in the engagement when Henry of Navarre defeated the Leaguers. Three times he rescued Lord Willoughby when unseated in the battle, and was himself severely wounded, lying all night on the battlefield. Surgeons despaired of his life, but he eventually recovered, although his health was so impaired that he could not continue his military career.

Returning to Tunstead Milton to take possession of his farm, Dickson found that his cousin, Jack Johnson, and his wife, had claimed the property on the assumption that he was dead. Although received with obvious coolness and reluctance, the ex-soldier was invited to spend the night at the farm, and, if local suspicions were correct, was murdered in his bed. Although the Johnsons thought that they had concealed their dastardly crime by burying the corpse on the premises, they were terrified one winter's night, less than a year following the murder, by the sudden appearance of the dead man's head. The wife was first to see the gruesome spectacle:

"What's that i' the nook, John?" she suddenly cried,
And shaking with terror they clearly espied
The head of Ned Dickson upright on the stone,
As wan and as ghastly as when he was done.

Many years passed away and the murderers fell,
By just retribution as ancient folk tell;
By a blow from her husband the woman was killed,
By the fall of an oak was Jack Johnson's blood spilled.

But the head of Ned Dickson still stood in the nook,
Though they tried to remove it by bell and by book;
Though wasted of skin and of flesh, still the skull
Will remain at its post till its weird be full.

On one occasion the skull was suggested as a show attraction at a social function. A writer says: "It was a fact that only a year or two ago the loan of 'Dickey' was requested for a side show and additional attraction to a bazaar being held in the Church schools at Chapel-en-le-Frith. His owners knowing, however, his mischievous reputation, consented only on the strict understanding that he was safely returned to his accustomed window corner before sunset. At this point negotiations were broken off, both sides feeling, probably, that they were best off as they were, so 'Dickey' did not enjoy the unaccustomed gaiety of a church bazaar!"

In a 1934 issue of the *Derbyshire Countryside*, Dr. L. du Garde Peach wrote of a short visit he paid to the farm, on which occasion he slept in a back room overlooking a small walled croft or garden. A week or two later, a French woman came to act as temporary housekeeper and occupied the same room. During the first night she was wakened by a feeling that something dreadful was happening in the back garden. So strong was the intuition that she got out of bed and peered through the window, and there saw two figures engaged in a desperate struggle in the moonlight. She was able to discern the form of a man who was in the act of strangling a young woman, when there was a sudden stifled scream and the two figures were blotted out by a cloud scudding across the face of the moon. Dr. Peach wrote: "The French housekeeper left next day. She had always known that she was psychic, but nothing would induce her to stay another night under the same roof as Dickie's skull."

There is a rival story to that which says that the skull was part of the anatomy of Ned Dickson, and this claims that it was the original property of one of two co-heiresses to the farm who was foully murdered and who expressed the dying wish that her bones should not be removed from the premises. This legend can be more readily vindicated than can the Trooper Dickson story. As far back as 1809 a writer contended "The skull has always been said to be that of a female, but why it should have been baptised with a name belonging to the male sex, seems somewhat anomalous." This challenge as to the masculinity of the frail fragments of mortality has been confirmed, I believe, by pathological examination, causing the Ned Dickson legend to totter and strengthening the co-heiress story, but the name "Dickey" still clings to the skull.

J. Castle Hall wrote: "Many years ago there lived here two sisters who were legatees of considerable property in the neighbourhood, including Tunstead Farm. For several years they lived very unhappily together; indeed, they quarrelled almost daily on who should be the final heiress of the house in which they lived. However, it is said that on her deathbed one of the sisters muttered continuously the words, 'My bones shall remain here for ever.' Tradition has it that for many years after her death the cottage was haunted, and owing to strange sounds became untenable until someone, remembering the dying words of the deceased owner, dug up her remains and brought the skull and placed it on a window-sill of the room in which the woman had died.

"According to the evidence of many local inhabitants, the house is peaceful and quiet while the skull remains there, but if it be removed the voices recur, and a voice is heard in the wind as the latter, with strange moanings, comes through the keyholes of every door in the house, saying, 'Fetch poor Dickie back. . . . Fetch poor Dickie back . . .,' and to this day the weird skull rests in the quiet corner of the window, and in the room a peculiar silence reigns."

A Mr. Lomas who occupied the farm during the 1880s had an experience before the death of his baby daughter. One night he was sitting alone in the kitchen, except for the baby in its cradle, when he heard someone coming downstairs and saw a female figure pass between his chair and the fireplace to bend over the cradle. Thinking that it was a servant, he warned her not to disturb the baby and said he would take the sleeping child to bed. But while he was speaking the figure vanished. On another occasion, a farmer tenant and his wife were returning home in a cart from which the woman had to descend and open and close each gate to allow the passage of the vehicle. Wearily the old woman exclaimed, "I wish Dickey would open the gates," whereupon each gate afterwards opened and then closed on its own volition.

When helping to write a book on Derbyshire walks some years ago, I entered into conversation with a workman at Shallcross Manor. The conversation began with a query concerning the mysterious Roosedyche, but eventually veered round to the famous "Piltdown Man of the Peak", when I learned that—as far as my informant knew—the skull had been built into a wall of the farm-house. Dickey is not unique in the Peak District as an amulet against evil, for we find several other instances of the same physical link connected with abstract hauntings. Dr. Addy tells of a skull which was kept on a window-sill at Dunscar Farm, near Castleton.

Another human skull is kept at Flagg Hall, and, like Dickey o' Tunstead, has become accepted as part of the valuation. Tradition tells of misfortune suffered in the event of its removal or abuse. It was formerly preserved beneath a glass case on the stairs. An attempt was once made to bury the skull in Chelmorton churchyard, but, upon reaching a point known as Chelmorton Thorn, the horses drawing the improvised hearse refused to proceed further. They stamped and reared as though confronted by some invisible presence, and the driver had to turn the vehicle round, return to the Hall and restore the rebellious skull to its accustomed place on the stairs. Mrs. Lomas, who formerly lived at the Hall, expressed the opinion that the skull was part of a human skeleton which was the professional property of a surgeon who once had a practice in the district and lived at the Hall. Such skeletons were often stolen from churchyards by "resurrectionists" who disposed of them to members of the medical profession for experimental purposes. A journalist visited the Hall and reported his experiences in a sensational article in which he described how fire flashed from the eyeless sockets of the skull, and how the grisly object persisted in performing such a violent jig that it was torn from his grasp.

An even stranger talisman was that of a pair of wooden clogs preserved at Thornylea Farm—nicknamed "Clog Hall"—not far from Tunstead. If removed from the farm, the tyrant clogs threatened ill-fortune for the occupants. Upon examining the clogs and finding them riddled with worm, one stout-hearted lady—aunt of the workman I met at Shallcross Manor—decided to risk retribution by applying her own ritual of exorcism and committed them to the fire. At Wheston Hall the removal of a model soldier from its accustomed place also threatened to ruin cattle and crops.

11. Chesterfield and District

IN 1675 a pamphlet, consisting of four pages, was printed and published in London. It had the intriguing title: "Strange and Terrible News from Chesterfield in Darbyshire: Being a full and true Relation of a horrible and terrible Ghost that was visibly seen on Sunday the 24th of January 1674. First in the Shape of a Dog, then a Woman, and afterwards a Man. Together with the discovery of some money that was hidden by Him in his Lifetime.

Richard Hobbs, Constable
James Knit, Constable
Joseph Wilson, Church-warden
Mr. Down, Gentleman."

The pamphlet recorded a series of strange happenings which began on Sunday night, the 24th January, 1674, when a couple of elderly residents were rudely disturbed from sleep. The cause of the disturbance was a loud hammering upon their bedroom door at nearly 3 o' clock in the morning. Clambering out of bed, the old man hastened to the door, but reeled back at the spectacle of "a Dog of great Stature, cole black colour, and most Terrible to behold, which presently vanished away with many horrible howlings and screechings. . . ."

Shaken with fright, the old man summoned the constable who made a fruitless search for the mysterious animal. The following night, a similar frantic knocking at the door heralded a different visitor—"a woman's shape, all bloody" which eventually disappeared to the accompaniment of blood-curdling sounds.

It was perhaps little surprise to the couple that the knocking should be repeated on the third night, whereupon the old man courageously opened the door to find a man of gigantic stature standing on the threshold. He spoke in gentle and kindly tones, however, to reassure the occupants of the bedroom and persuaded the old man to accompany him without fear of molestation. Reaching a field not far from his home, the man was shown a hidden hoard of money which, the spectre explained, he had stolen during a dishonest lifetime. He pleaded that the old man would restore the hidden wealth to those to whom it rightfully belonged. The old man forthwith carried out the instructions and peace was restored to his household.

A bank in New Square, Chesterfield, was formerly the residence of a certain Dr. Jones who incorrectly named it "The Old Manor House." It had black oak panelling, and was re-built on similar lines to the original late Tudor or early Stuart architecture. During the early years of the 19th century, a resident of this house described the circumstances in which her aunt saw the ghost of a small child in an upstairs room or corridor. Thinking the occurrence rather strange and wondering how the little stranger came to be in the house, she stooped to pick up the child and was horrified when her arms passed through the ethereal body. So great was her consternation that she fled from the spot and descended the stairs, taking each flight of seven at a single stride. The same person related an experience concerning her grandmother who heard a ghost with clanking chain walking across the floor of the hall and into the dining-room where she was awaiting the arrival of her husband—a doctor. Although she took the precaution of locking the room—presumably to imprison the fettered phantom—this proved no deterrent to the ghostly intruder and it noisily clanked out of the room again.

A sister of this same lady saw something "horrifying and indescribable" in this house, but applied her own ritual of exorcism by flinging a Bible at it.

Chesterfield had a house haunted by an unaccountable ringing of its bell system in the 1830s. The house was called "Rosehill" and stood on the site now occupied by the Town Hall. Its occupant at the time was Mr. James Ashwell who became tenant about the year 1830. After some time had elapsed, all the bells in the house developed the habit of ringing on their own volition; an occurrence which usually took place in the evening. Suspicion was at first centred upon mischievous servants, but they were absolved from blame when the bells rang violently at a time when it was proved that they could not possibly have been responsible for the operation. New bells were installed to try to effect a remedy, but these continued the mysterious exercise in campanology, and even persisted when the wires were severed!

Sometimes there would be a pause lasting for several months, but then the ringing would be resumed to the annoyance of the occupants. Electrical and wind experiments were tried in order to explain the behaviour of the bells, but without success. Scientists who came from as far away as London, and the friends of Mr. Ashwell, had to acknowledge themselves baffled by the uncanny circumstances, and, after enduring the nuisance for some years, Mr. Ashwell reluctantly vacated the premises and "Rosehill" was never again occupied.

One witness testified that "all the bells rang unaccountably at one time or another, never earlier than 5 a.m. and never later than 11 p.m. They continued to ring even after the wires connecting them with their pulls had been severed. The oscillation in each case was like that of a pendulum—not a decreasing one. A bell, unattached to any wire, was put up one Saturday evening. As if of its own accord, it began to ring within half an hour. In the same way, the moveable shutter bells on the parlour window inside shutters rang even when this apartment was unoccupied, and indeed its door securely locked. All the bells hung well out of reach, and in a house so substantially built that no one was as much as aware of the most violent gale which might be raging without. All attempts to detect any mischievous tampering with them proved unavailing.

"An amusing incident occurred when a bell-hanger came to re-connect the wires which had been cut in the hope of finding a solution. One of the bells began to ring defiantly in his face. He instantly dropped down the ladder and, without even collecting his tools, fled, crying that Satan was in the bells, and he would have no more to do with them. The ringings in this old Derbyshire house, which had long been regarded as haunted, continued intermittently for about eighteen months. On several occasions, James Ashwell, the owner, seized an oscillating bell, thus compelling a cessation of its ringing. But it immediately resumed whenever he released his hold of it. Several of his servants left his employment in alarm, owing to the bells' behaviour; and so unenviable a reputation did the house acquire that foot passengers using the public pathway close by it now made a detour to avoid it. At one stage in Mr. Ashwell's investigations as to the cause for this persistent annoyance, he altered, on two or three occasions, the order in which the bells hung. He now observed that, when they resumed their uncanny ringing, a particular bell always took the lead. Three other bells followed in the same order, irrespective of the order in which he hung them."

The Hagge is a fine Jacobean mansion situated a mile and a half west of Staveley. Records say that it was built by Sir Peter Freschville as a shooting lodge, a dower house, or an annexe to Staveley Hall. From the leaded roof of the tall, square, two-storeyed porch, the ladies are said to have watched the progress of the hunt in a clearing made in the foreground for this purpose. Some writers assign the date of the mansion to the latter half of the 16th century, and this claim is supported by an entry in Staveley Parish Register referring to Thomas Hitch who resided at the Hagge in 1618. It is now a farmhouse.

The Hagge is reputed to be haunted by a White Lady, and Mr. C. C. Handford, who perhaps has a more intimate knowledge of the locality than any other historian, says: "It was in this house that Frances, daughter of Lord John Freschville and his second wife, Sarah Harrington (one time maid of honour to Queen Henrietta

The Hagge, near Staveley

Maria) was born on 1st November, 1638. Much is recorded of this lady and tradition has it that she is the mysterious 'White Lady' associated with the Hagge. Certain it was that she became the wife of Colonel Culpepper (Thomas), or Colepepper, a creature of the Court of James II, who seems to have spent much of his time in the pursuit of pleasure . . ." It was this Culpepper whom the Earl of Devonshire assaulted at Court for an imagined insolent glance, grasping the offender firmly by the nose and leading him out of the room to belabour him with the head of his cane; an action which resulted in a fine of £30,000 (which he never paid) and an imprisonment from which he escaped to Chatsworth.

During the occupation of the Hagge by the late Mr. Crawshaw, the White Lady was seen by an Irish visitor who had never previously been to the house, and who had never heard of its being haunted. On the morning after his arrival, the Irishman glanced curiously round the breakfast table and enquired whether the lady in white would not be joining them for the meal. He had passed her on the stairs the previous night! About the year 1863, Mrs.

H. Swift—a local poetess—wrote the following verses about the ghostly White Lady:

No steeds wait in that courtyard
Obedient to the rein,
But a garden blooms in beauty
When summer decks the plain.

Thence as you cross the entrance hall
To ascend the oaken stair,
Fear not to meet the lady
Who hath oft-times lingered there.

In cloak and hat of antique guise,
And robes of purest white,
She vanish'd from the gazer's sight
E'en in the noontide light.

'Twas Christmas; like a traveller
From the postern gate she passed,
When lights were blazing in the hall
And sleet fell thick and fast.

Surely she was a blessed sprite
Who then did church-ward go,
Nor traces left of passing steps
Upon the stainless snow.

A serving man obeisance made
As to one of mortal mould,
With look unchanged she passed him by,
Her eyes were fixed and cold.

None stayed her step, none questioned her,
For her lips were mute and pale,
And a snow-white greyhound followed,
Fleet as the passing gale.

She was not seen when mirth and song
Ascended to the roof;
She came not with the bridal guests
In her robes of heavenly woof.

They glimmered through the midnight gloom
Ere the last of a name and race
Was borne away from her lonely couch
To the grave's cold resting place.

The Hagge was once famous for its "mandrake tree"—a venerable oak which tradition claimed had been a focal point of Druid worship and ritual, and which was guarded by a vicious ogre. It was said to be the only oak in Derbyshire which bore mistletoe, having been known to yield the mystic parasite as far back as the reign of Charles II and as recently as 1808. It had the sinister reputation of being semi-human, screaming and bleeding when its branches were severed, and even speaking with the voice of prophetic doom! The tree was chained together and supported by a timber fence, then, later, by a mound of earth and stone, but on December 12th, 1883, it became the victim of a terrible gale and was blown down.

The following incident was reported in the Sheffield evening newspaper, *The Star*, during November, 1958. Mr. John McGoary, an Irishman working in the Shirebrook Colliery, saw a ghost and fainted. "All I will say now is that I saw a vision and a light," said Mr. McGoary. "The vision went past me: it looked like Wilfred Hales." Another miner, Mr. Keith Plant, also claimed to have seen the spectre and also recognised it as the shade of Wilfred Hales who, at the age of thirty, had collapsed and died in the January of 1955. The circumstance caused considerable comment among the 2,000 men employed at the colliery, and the management complained that production was being seriously retarded by the alleged ghost.

In the files of the above newspaper, which I was privileged to examine, I found a record concerning mysterious happenings at the "Sun Inn", Chatsworth Road, Chesterfield. These occurred around midnight during the November of 1957. The landlord, Mr. Vincent Holmes, described how crates of beer had been found smashed and barrels moved out of place in the cellar, even though the door had been locked all night. Footsteps were heard padding around at intervals. The happenings were linked with the legend of a ghostly coachman who, 200 years ago, was murdered and his body thrown down a well in the cellar of this 300-years-old inn.

Eerie noises and footsteps were also heard in 1960 at the "Nag's Head", Newbold, according to the then landlord, Mr. Albert Richards, and his daughter, Carol. Miss Richards described the footsteps as being heavy and quick. The movements were believed to have some connection with the seven-centuries-old Catholic Chapel at the rear of the premises.

Bolsover Castle, with its long pageant of history, may well be concluded to be a place which would attract visitors from the past as well as from the present. In his *Rambles among the Hills*, Louis J. Jennings records the impressions formed during a visit to the castle through which he was conducted by an old woman. "We went downstairs, below the house itself, to the cellars and passages which are said to be the remains of the Norman structure. There was a high vaulted roof to the chamber now used as a kitchen, and an ancient stone passage connected it with a sort of crypt, beneath which, as the old woman said—and I can neither verify nor disprove her account, but am content to take it as I received it—is a church, never opened since the days of William de Peverell, or Peveril, son of William the Conqueror. Our voices had a hollow sound; my footsteps awakened echoes from every corner. There must be some large empty space beneath the stone floor, but what it was used for in other days no one seems to know. They say it has never been opened or examined. The chamber in which I stood was sufficiently strange—it might have been a wizard's cave, and all the world alseep. 'This,' I said in jest, 'is where all your noises and ghosts come from.' But the old woman answered very seriously, 'It is, sir; and when the family are here the servants sometimes will not come down except by twos and threes. Oh, many people have seen things here besides me. Something bad has been done here, sir, and when they open that church below they'll find it out. Just where you stand, by that door, I have several times seen a lady and gentleman—only for a moment or two, for they come like a flash. When I have been sitting in the kitchen, not thinking of any such thing, they stood there—the gentleman with ruffles on, the lady with a scarf round her waist. I never believed in ghosts, but I have seen *them*. I am used to it now, and don't mind it. But we do not like the noises, because they disturb us. Not long ago my husband, who comes here at night, and I, could not sleep at all, and we thought at last that somebody had got shut up in the castle, for some children had been here that day. So we lit a candle and went all over it, but there was nothing, only the noises following us, and keeping on worse than ever after we left the rooms, though they stopped while we were in them.' "

After I had been speaking at Chesterfield Townswomen's Guild on the subject of "Derbyshire Ghost Stories", a member of the audience who lives at nearby Sutton Wood—although protesting that she was no public speaker, and greatly abashed to find herself on her feet—spontaneously volunteered to tell a personal story of the spectre of a monk which she and several relatives and friends had seen in their locality. Dressed in conventional habit, the monk was distinctly recognisable by the fact that he was wearing a golden cross, perhaps as emblem of office or status. He had been seen by the witness's husband who had walked in silence alongside the robed figure until it suddenly disappeared through a hedge. Still unconvinced of the "reality" of the figure, he had visited the spot on several successive nights to try to prove to himself that it could only have been a shadow.

The speaker's brother, returning from shift-work one morning about 2 a.m., mistook the figure for that of a woman who he assumed had been to a doctor or on some other urgent errand. Not wishing to startle the woman, he was pondering whether to acquaint her of his presence with a formal "goodnight", or to hurry past without speaking, when his problem was solved by the figure vanishing as he drew nearer. The speaker, and some friends present at the meeting, all testified to having seen the monk with the golden cross.

Acknowledgements

IN making acknowledgements, I would like to thank so many people who have opened their hearts and homes to me while collecting material for this book, and to the Derbyshire Federation of Womens' Institutes for the original inspiration and continued encouragement. I must have spoken at upwards of two hundred meetings on this subject, and have considerable engagements in the future.

I am particularly grateful to Mr. E. Hector Kyme, a fastidious photographer whose viewfinder is a crystal ball of magic, marvel and mystery. Although preoccupied with reporting for publication his mammoth "after retirement" walk from the north-west of Scotland to Dover, and under pressure for illustrative material from more professional journalists than myself, he willingly placed his equipment, experience and time at my disposal during several memorable trips to different parts of Derbyshire. There is no need for me to seek flattering phraseology to describe his artistry; this will be self-evident even to those who may not consciously be connoisseurs of camera craftsmanship. And I must explain that his services have been contributed, not on a basis of finance so much as on one of friendship.

Thanks are also due to the editors of such journals as "Derbyshire Life & Countryside," "The Star," "The Sheffield Telegraph," "The Derbyshire Times" and "The Buxton Advertiser" who have so willingly allowed access to their respective files and given permission to publish information they contain.